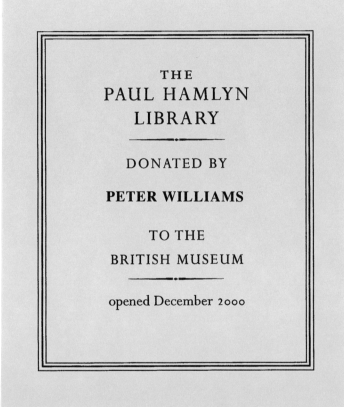

Churches the Victorians Forgot

Mark Chatfield

Churches the Victorians Forgot

Moorland Publishing

British Library Cataloguing in Publication Data
Chatfield, Mark
  Churches the Victorians forgot.
  1. Churches — England
  I. Title
942 DA660

ISBN 0 86190 328 5

First Edition 1979
Revised Second Edition 1989

To Binsey Church, Oxford, my childhood playground,
where I first learned to love old churches.

Printed and bound in Great Britain by
Richard Clay Ltd, Bungay, Suffolk.

Published by
Moorland Publishing Co Ltd,
Moor Farm Road West,
Ashbourne, Derbys DE6 1HD.

Foreword

I am most grateful to Moorland Publishing Company for offering, in a completely unsolicited way, to reissue this book. It has been said on more than one occasion that everyone has a book inside them; this is undoubtedly mine! An acquaintance with two or three unrestored 'prayer-book' churches led to a burning desire to seek out all such survivors in England. The acceptance of the project came as an intoxicating challenge to fulfill that desire. So I set off, accompanied by camera and pen, on a kind of whistle-stop tour, enticed into remote corners by the lure of box pew, decked pulpit, gallery and plastered roof. Armed with a bedrock of descriptions of potentially archetypal interiors from Pevsner's *Buildings of England*, I tramped along tracks, knocked upon doors for keys and breathtakingly opened ancient doors in anticipation of hopes consummated. It is a tribute to that most remarkable of men that in one instance only did his description of a church and its fittings fail to send my steps thither, a mistake rectified too late for inclusion in the first edition. The excursion proved to be, on the whole, a happy odyssey of discovering churches tended and cared for. Occasionally sadness prevailed; Shireshead, which had been sold off as a hall for the local scouts, its furnishings removed. Then there was that infamous trio Pilling, Skelton and, above all, Goltho, derelict in each case, the latter standing empty and abandoned, its fittings removed, its walls disfigured by mindless graffiti. Yet, here I can record a happy ending, for all three are now with the Redundant Churches Fund and have been made whole again, their wounds healed.

It is now twelve years since I undertook this pilgrimage through an older England. I have revisited hardly any of these churches, more from a fear of change than anything else, but I have acquainted myself with, and photographed, many more of varying character. Have my views concerning the relative merits of these "forgotten" churches changed? In essence, no. Whilst I recognize that there exist many architecturally more valuable buildings, in terms of untouched character and visual poetry, of an edifice breathing as a living thing, I still believe that those described herein represent the cream of England's village churches.

Mark Chatfield
Faringdon, 1989

Acknowledgements

In preparing the material for this updated reprint I forwarded copies of the original text to the relevant incumbents and to the Redundant Churches Fund. I am grateful to all those vicars and rectors who took time to comment and especially to those who sent me far more information than I had asked for. A special thank you to Mr Howard Colvin for thoughts on Shobdon, the authorship of which remains a mystery as before. A very special thanks goes to Messrs Anthony Barnes and John Bowles, respectively Director and Secretary of the Redundant Churches Fund, for much annotated comment upon my descriptions of the churches now in their care.

Contents

Introduction

In a quiet corner of Lincolnshire lies the hamlet of Langton-by-Partney. It consists of a church, a former rectory, a cottage orné, and a few other dwellings. The church, concealed by a screen of trees, is an odd-looking affair with brick walls, a deeply-eaved roof, clear-glazed windows, and a strange octagonal bellcote. It is, indeed, unconventional enough to lead the experienced explorer of churches to suspect that within its walls may lurk items of uncommon interest. A supposition of this kind can often lead to disappointment, but at Langton all expectations are rewarded in full measure. Stepping into the interior one is immediately transported back in time to the world of eighteenth-century Protestantism. The furnishings have not changed since the close of the Georgian epoch. Seating is provided by box pews arranged longitudinally as in a college chapel; a splendid three-decker pulpit rises above them half-way along one side; there is a west gallery where once the musicians gathered; the roof is plastered and ceiled; the altar is backed by a beautiful apsidal reredos of wood; and the font is squeezed into the corner by the communion rail.

Langton-by-Partney serves as an introduction to those churches which form the subject of this book. They are the churches the Victorians forgot, the churches which escaped the flood of restoration carried out during the decades after 1840. Opening a window upon the physical setting of the Protestant liturgy, these interiors provide us with our only tangible link with two and a half centuries of 'prayer-book' worship. These unrestored buildings exist today because they fortuitously escaped the effects of the Tractarians' reforming zeal. The majority are to be found in country parishes with scattered populations formerly too poor to finance costly restorations, and in parishes remote from the centres of liturgical reform. Several were simply abandoned and replaced by new buildings (perhaps more conveniently located), only to be rehabilitated when appreciation of their intrinsic qualities had been fully realized. Didmarton, Gloucestershire, is one church which underwent this process of suspended animation. Others came through the holocaust by the skin of their teeth. Inglesham, Wiltshire, was especially fortunate in that the great William Morris kept a discerning and protective eye upon a necessary but gentle restoration. The pristine state of St John, Leeds, with its gorgeous Carolean woodwork, is, however, the result of an eleventh hour protest against despoilation (though even here some changes were made).

St John is exceptional in that it is a town church. As already mentioned, the majority of these churches occur in rural areas, although several are in villages which became ensnared in nineteenth and twentieth century urban expansion (eg, Beauchief on the fringe of Sheffield). St John, however, is in the centre of Leeds, a surprising survival in so eminently Victorian a town, the proud possessor of that most grand of all nineteenth-century town halls. On the whole, though, town parishes were wealthy, and so extensive restoration and re-equipping took place almost everywhere. It is also true that in general town churches allied themselves more readily with the High Church camp. The liturgical changes demanded by the Tractarian Movement ostensibly necessitated a re-arrangement of furnishings, and such substantial items as box pews, galleries, etc, could only be adapted to the new requirements with difficulty. So out they had to go, to be replaced by Gothic-style woodwork, nearly all of it less homogeneous, less honest and less convincing. Yet it would have been possible to conduct a High Church service in a 'prayer-book' interior; the real reason for discarding these homely settings was, of course, not practical but doctrinal.

High or Low Church, Tractarians, ecclesiology — to many readers, no doubt, these terms will appear obscure, but before we discuss them in greater detail an attempt at portraying a typical church interior as it existed at the dawn of the Reformation must be made. This is necessary in order to understand, on the one hand, the changes created by the English prayer book of 1549 and, on the other, the reverse process initiated by the Tractarians and others from about 1840.

If we could return to the early years of Henry VIII's reign and enter a parish church, the contrast between its interior and that of a church today would be immediately apparent; to our church-going ancestors of the seventeenth and eighteenth centuries it would come as a profound shock. The most striking impression would be the exploitation of colour. It was everywhere: on capitals, mouldings, walls and statues, on hangings, and in the windows. Large areas of walling were covered with paintings depicting biblical stories, scenes of incidents in the lives of saints, moralities, etc, and these were echoed by glowing stained glass that spread a 'dim religious glow' (to use Pugin's phrase) throughout the building. A screen, usually of wood but sometimes of stone, stood beneath the chancel arch, forming a clear division between nave and chancel. This screen supported a gilded and painted statue of the crucified Christ (the rood) and there might be other screens between the chancel and its chapels and across aisles or transepts. Numerous altars were placed about the building, each with its own lamp burning, where private masses were said for the souls of the departed. The subdued lighting punctuated by the flickering lamps, and the frequent comings and goings of priests, created a highly-charged atmosphere of mystery and awe.

This environment of ritual and not a little superstition was swept away at the Reformation by a new force much more austere, yet equally dogmatic and single-minded. The conversion of half Europe from a Catholic to a Protestant faith is familiar and hardly needs retelling. Martin Luther's is a household name, but the Reformation was the product of diverse origins and emanated from many quarters. The first link in the chain which eventually led to the exclusion of Catholicism from English life was forged by the Dissolution of the Monasteries, a secular, rather than a religious, act. These self-contained, enclosed worlds had grown senile yet extremely powerful. Many had become rich through gifts of land and the possession of so-called relics, often no more than a collection of crumbling bones or filty rags. Their role as sanctuaries of learning had largely been negated by the growth of secular education. Thus, while the Dissolution was chiefly the act of a jealous and greedy king, some reform through legislation would have become inevitable. Be that as it may, the immediate result was that a vast body of powerful Catholic influence was, at a stroke, swept away.

Link number two was the King's divorce of his Catholic queen, Catherine of Aragon, and his subsequent marriage to Anne Boleyn. These events took place in 1533 and resulted in the king being ex-communicated by the Pope. Henry then declared himself supreme head of the English Church, or *Fide Defensor*, a title that had been conferred upon him some years earlier, paradoxically, by a Pope in gratitude for his having written a book on Catholic doctrine. Henry, indeed, remained essentially loyal to these doctrines, and it was not until the accession of Edward VI in 1547 that the final break with Rome occurred. The Boy King was a convinced Lutheran and it was he who established the Protestant Church of England, dissolving the chantries and guilds in 1547-8 and issuing the first English prayer-books.

What effect did these events have on the interiors of churches in the second half of the sixteenth century? The first changes were almost all negative ones. During the reign of Edward VI a wave of iconoclasm swept across the country, destroying images, discarding vestments, and generally eliminating as much imagery as possible. To the more extreme Protestants (eg, the Calvinists) all images and pictures were idolatrous; consequently many beautiful statues and stained glass windows were wantonly destroyed. Representations of Christ and the Virgin were especially sought out; not one English rood survives in anything but a fragmentary state. Colour disappeared from interiors as wall paintings were whitewashed over and replaced by texts from the bible. Thus, by the time Elizabeth came to the throne, our medieval churches stood bare and empty, stripped of their finery, their services combined and greatly reduced in number.

The English prayer book of 1549 has too often been blamed for this iconoclasm; rather it was the result of Calvinist and other Puritan elements who were very influential in later sixteenth century England. Also, as with any ideological revolution, the visual manifestations of the displaced ideology tend to be disfigured and destroyed as a symbolic act of purification. Thus it was during the reign of Edward VI. In Elizabeth's time something was done to redress these excesses but the chief problem facing the reformers was how to adapt the legacy of medieval churches to the liturgical requirements of the 1549 prayer book. The pre-Reformation services were very different from those of the Anglican church today and, one might say, the absolute converse of those current between about 1558 and about 1840. To begin with, the laity were discouraged from entering the chancel, except for special festivals. Indeed, they hardly took part in the services at all; communion, for example, was celebrated by the clergy, the laity watching from the nave. Services were conducted in Latin, except for the sermon. Frequent services were held daily, the laity often entered and left while they were in progress, and when services were not taking place naves were used for all kinds of secular activities.

The 1549 prayer book required that the laity take part in all aspects of the services, that Matins and Evensong should be conducted from the chancel, and that the Lesson was to be read so that all could hear. It did not, however, say anything as to the position or nature of the altar, but during Edward's short reign Hooper and Ridley campaigned for the replacement of stone altars by wooden tables. Their persistence paid off, for in 1550 all bishops were ordered to replace the stone altars in their dioceses with wooden tables, and in Easter of that year the table

in Old St Paul's was being placed lengthwise in the choir. In 1552, for the first time, the prayer book used the term 'table'. Then came the brief Catholic interlude of Mary's reign.

In 1560 Elizabeth I ordered that the Ten Commandments, Lord's Prayer, Creed, etc, be set up at the east end, and in 1561 that screens were to be retained but the loft, etc, removed. Communion tables were to be covered and not left bare and it was recommended that the Royal Arms be placed above the screen or in some other convenient place. It was not until 1660, however, that the placing of the Royal Arms in churches became compulsory. Thus, shortly after the accession of Elizabeth I began the gradual transformation of the former Catholic interior to meet the requirements of the new Protestant liturgy. Still nothing was said as to where the communion table should stand; the Puritans favoured a lengthwise position in the centre of the chancel (as it still exists at Hailes, Gloucestershire). Others preferred to bring the table into the nave for the celebration and return it to the east end afterwards. Gradually, the chancel fell out of use, except for communion, and the whole service was conducted from the pulpit, hence the development of the three-decker pulpit, the priest occupying the middle tier except during the sermon, which he delivered from the upper tier. The clerk led the responses from the bottom tier.

The next problem was seating; with the exceptions of East Anglia and the South-West few areas had consistently provided their churches with seats. Now, for much of the service, the congregation would require seats. In Devon and Cornwall the tradition of medieval-style benches continued right into the 1570s, and among our 'prayer-book' churches will be noted some where, well into the seventeenth century, open benches were preferred (eg, Tushingham of 1689-91). But gradually the enclosed box pew with door and seats around three sides became *de rigueur*, culminating, perhaps, in those set logitudinally like the stalls in a college chapel (eg, Well, of 1733). The pews tended to be centred upon the pulpit, thus creating, where no chancel arch existed, the auditory type of interior. Such churches, naturally enough, are mainly purpose-built seventeenth and eighteenth-century buildings (though Old Dilton, Wiltshire, is a good example of a medieval church adapted). The exemplar is King's Norton, Leicestershire, the earliest now extant Langley Chapel, Shropshire (about 1601).

During the 1630s William Laud, made Archbishop of Canterbury in 1633, and the High Church party, tried to introduce more ritual into the services. Laud encouraged the protection of a *permanently-placed* east altar by the installation of the now familiar communion rail. The primary purpose of this rail, with its rather closely spaced balusters, was to keep dogs out of the sanctuary; that it became a convenient adjunct for the kneeling communicants was of secondary importance. Previously, the communicants had either knelt around the table itself or in specially provided pews (not stalls in the modern sense). Regarding interiors in general, the culmination of this phase could be said to be the installation in certain County Durham churches of Gothic-style furnishings under Bishop Cosin. At Brancepeth, for example, medieval-type choir stalls *were* introduced. But the finest Laudian interior is undoubtedly Staunton Harold in Leicestershire, built, paradoxically, during the Commonwealth. Yet ten years before this church was begun, ie, in 1643, Parliament passed an ordinance abolishing all east altars and communion rails. How many of the latter were destroyed cannot be ascertained; certainly quite a number of pre-Commonwealth rails survive (eg, Brooke, Rutland). With the Restoration things settled down and by the end of the eighteenth century every Anglican church must have been equipped with a set of 'prayer-book' furnishings in one arrangement or another.

Even a cursory glance at the photographs will reveal the widely varying characteristics of these interiors. Yet there exist only three basic layouts; the furnishings are composed around one, two or three liturgical centres. The type with three centres has its altar, pulpit and font clearly segregated, the font somewhere near the west end, the pulpit either near the chancel arch or screen or half-way down one side. Two-centre interiors possess a combination of either pulpit and font (eg, Minstead, Hampshire), pulpit and altar (eg, Beauchief, West Riding), or altar and font (eg, Langton-by-Partney, Lincolnshire). Lastly, the single-centre type has pulpit, font and altar grouped together at the east end (eg, Shobdon, Herefordshire). This, from the liturgical point of view, is the most satisfactory, but it is not always the most successful visually. It all depends on the character and harmony of the furnishings *in toto*.

During the decade from 1830 to 1840 a new breeze began to blow which was eventually to attain gale-force proportions and in doing so swept away the majority of 'prayer-book' interiors. The first salvo was fired by Pugin in his *Contrasts*, published in 1836. In it he portrayed idealized medieval townscapes contrasted against the squalid and disfigured industrial towns of his own day. In 1841 came his *True Principles of Christian Architecture* in which he argued that to be Christian was to be Pointed (ie, Gothic) and to be Pointed was to be Christian. Therefore, all churches had to be Gothic, but not just any Gothic. Perpendicular was degenerate, Early English immature; the 'correct' style was the bar tracery from Westminster Abbey (about 1245) to the early fourteenth century. He was also concerned about furnishings, and he was the first architect to design correct medieval-style churches.

Meanwhile, the Tractarian Movement had been born, centred upon Oxford, and led by John Newman, who later became a Catholic (as did Pugin). The Tractarians wished to revive ancient ritual and to do so required churches in which it could be accurately performed, churches with proper altars and deep chancels. Over in Cambridge, the Camden Society was founded in 1839 to further these aims and also ecclesiology in general. This society became immensely influential and its journal, *The Ecclesiologist*, first published in 1841, virtually dictated the whole course of church building, restoration and re-equipping for the succeeding fifty years. It gave advice to the clergy as to how they could 'improve' and re-arrange their churches, generously supported its favourite architects and unswervingly condemned those would would not conform. Camdenians' immense influence is still manifest today in nearly every Anglican church. What is regarded as a 'typical' church interior does not pre-date, at least in its layout, the 1840s, except, that is, for the precious survival of our seventy-odd 'prayer-book' churches described herein and indicated by an asterisk in the gazeteer. The latter lists a further sixty-five churches whose interiors are reasonably untouched, which means that, out of something like eight thousand pre-Victorian churches in England, only about 140 retain interiors that, historically at any rate, can be regarded as truly 'Anglican'.

Note: the old county names are used throughout. The new counties are disliked by everyone except the bureaucrats who created them and have little to do with a thousand years of English history. Also, all existing major topographical guides still use the old names. Grid Reference numbers are given for each church so that its location may be found on the One Inch or 1:50,000 Ordnance Survey maps.

Hamstead Marshall

Hamstead Marshall church can be approached from two directions, *viz*, the west and north-east. From either the building remains concealed until the very last moment, creating an element of surprise. The lane winds upwards out of the Kennet Valley, past a white, octagonal canal house; then a dark clump of trees rises above the crest. That is all, and an approach from the opposite direction, along the ridge from the west, reveals only a substantial and seemingly endless wall, punctuated occasionally by gatepiers. The church, indeed, lies back beyond the trees, which shield it from the passer-by. It is the tower which presents itself first to the visitor as he ascends the path, a red brick tower, and this material is the *leitmotif* of Hamstead Marshall. Of brick the rambling wall along the lane, the wall surrounding the churchyard and the pairs of gatepiers standing like muted sentinels upon formerly prosperous lawns. Visually, the chief contrast lies between this uniformity of hue and texture and the varied green of the foliage around. The whole is bathed in an air of melancholy, a half-deserted mien engendered by memories of the now vanished, yet once proud, mansion of the Earls Craven.

The church is medieval, with a nave and chancel dating in its bones from the ending of the twelfth century. Of this time only the plain, round-arched south doorway remains, all other original features having been replaced during subsequent periods. This simple two-celled plan remained unchanged until about 1350 when a north aisle was added. Of its windows, those to the east and west are, with their cheerful, star-like tracery design, not only visually attractive but also historically instructive. The tracery includes both the reticulation motif of the Decorated style and the characteristic rectilinear panels of the Perpendicular period. This combination of motifs from two stylistic epochs, which occurs only infrequently, proves that the divide between Decorated and Perpendicular is not always so clearly demarcated as is sometimes supposed. No further major changes took place before the Reformation; some new straight-headed windows were inserted in the nave and chancel during the early sixteenth century, but otherwise the building's character was not altered until the eighteenth century when a west tower was built. Of course, this may have replaced a medieval tower but no evidence survives. Taken all-in-all, the church's exterior is not a particularly attractive one. The tower is rather bald and lifeless and the flint walls of the other parts display a hardness that is, perhaps, characteristic of this material. Also, the south side looks over-restored and the porch itself is Victorian.

On stepping inside, however, one enters a different world. The few architectural features are utterly subordinated by the visual impact of the furnishings. The botched and shapeless forms of arcade and chancel arch cannot even begin to compete with the feeling of solid craftsmanship engendered by so much stately woodwork. Nevertheless, their salient points need to be recorded. The arcade conforms in date to the aisle but repairs of the seventeenth century may have altered its character. It will be immediately obvious to everyone that the arches do not fit the responds with their polygonal shafts and moulded capitals. The *Victoria County History* suggests, in fact, that the arches consist mainly of plaster. As for the chancel arch, though it may have originally dated from the late twelfth century, its present curious pseudo-ogee shape must surely be the result of seventeenth century reconstruction. In marked contrast, the furnishings, including the ample, spreading, compartmented box pews, the rich magnificence of the pulpit, and the lofty restraint of the reredos, appear dignified indeed. They are also extremely harmonious, especially in their colouring, with browns and creams dominant. Attention must

Pulpit: detail

also be drawn to the crisp cross lighting in the chancel brought about by the lack of windows in the north and east walls. The east window was shown as being already bricked up in one of Kip's engravings published before 1709, so the present reredos, which must be late eighteenth century, replaces an earlier one. Only one incongruous feature exists within this interior of oak and plaster; the roundel with the Virgin and Child above the altar. It is, of course, completely anti-Protestant in feeling and conception.

Font: Early C17; octagonal; plain; possibly of plaster.
Font Cover: Early C17; openwork consisting of a turned central shaft and S-shaped arms.
Pulpit (with tester): Given in 1622 by Dorothy, Lady Parry; a two-decker; the clerk's part has plain panelling and a little arabesque decoration; the pulpit proper has blank arches and rich arabesque; the tester has a fluted canopy with a pendant.
Communion Table: C17; with turned legs.
Communion Rail: c1700, with turned balusters.
Box Pews: C18; all have two tiers of plain panelling; one (probably the squire's pew) has a raised back with pierced fretwork designs.
West Gallery: C18; on rather stout Tuscan columns; plainly panelled front.
Reredos: Late C18; tripartite arrangement with simple arched panels divided by pairs of extremely attenuated columns; deep architrave above; the texts have disappeared.

Hamstead Marshall: *Interior looking east*

Buckinghamshire SP846463

Gayhurst

As one approaches across the rough parkland, church and house resolve themselves into a visually stunning group, the house severe yet noble, the church rich and livelier. This organic interweaving of a house and a church, the dual symbols of Church and State, occurs happily often in England, and we shall meet it again later on. The buidings occupy an elevated position and look southwards across a copse to a lake-filled

Exterior from the south-east

13

Interior looking east

valley. This was laid out by Capability Brown but the lakes, or rather outsized ponds, do not form a picture with the architecture as they do at, eg, Staunton Harold or Well. The churchyard bears a Romantic aspect, with the trees, including a pine, overshadowing, and the wilder seclusion on the north side. Yet, to the west all is serene lawn.

The church was built in 1728 by an unknown architect, but as its motifs link up with the age of Wren, rather than with the new Palladianism, he was probably a local mason-builder. Such a man would be just one step behind the fashionable leaders. On the other hand, this kind of authorship imparts a robust craftsmanship quality that often produces a powerful individuality, as indeed it does here at Gayhurst. The building consists of a sturdy tower, a broad and stately nave, and a lower, narrower chancel. The tower is divided into two-and-a-half stages, the lower with evenly rusticated angle pilasters, the upper with plainly panelled pilasters. These last are connected by a string-course which links up with the abaci of the bell-openings. The latter push up into the plain and narrow half-stage above. The ground stage has a doorway with a surround of even rustication, a window over with Y-tracery, and round-arched niches north and south. The bell-openings have, again, Y-tracery, and below them occur large hexagons. This Y-tracery represents an interesting early case of Gothic Revival. Stylistically, it belongs to Wren's occasional excursions into medievalism, rather than to the 'modern Gothick' of Kent, etc. The tower is crowned by a recessed lead cupola with round-arched openings segregated by attached balusters and an ogee dome with finial. Corner pinnacles take the form of flaming torches.

The nave presents a symmetrical composition to the south, a typically Palladian composition only in the way the motifs build up towards the centre. They also appear as if attached to an inert wall instead of growing organically out of it as they would in a building of Vanbrugh or Hawksmoor. The angles have evenly rusticated pilasters as on the tower; then come Ionic pilasters and, finally, attached Ionic columns carrying a pediment. These stand upon high bases partly rusticated. The doorway has a round arch and a separate segmental pediment higher up connected to it by an eared frame. This frame is so lightly indicated, and the pediment so bold, that the latter remains visually firmly detached. It is a curious Mannerist device. The windows are round-arched with plain keystones, abaci and aprons. Above them occur plain, raised, rectangular panels. A rusticated base runs all along. On the north side the centre bay is even more idiosyncratic. It projects and is completely rusticated. Above the doorway occurs a pedimental gable, again detached, and above that a broad segmental pediment. This striking composition is ruined by the heating flue. The chancel has windows as before, the same angle pilasters, and a niche in the east wall as in the tower.

The interior is spacious and richly appointed — ceilings, reredos and monument all competing for attention. In its way, Gayhurst is the twin of Avington in Hampshire, but there exist several points of divergence. Gayhurst is certainly superior in its architectural enrichment. Avington, conversely, has a much more satisfactory *ensemble* of furnishings. At Gayhurst, two or three things detract, notably the lack of a gallery, the fussy infilling of the tower arch (not original), and the muddle around the pulpit. There is also a superfluity of posters; surely their humane messages could be proclaimed in a visually more acceptable manner. One further point: the heating is by hot air, and the mechanism fills the church with a continuous humming and rushing sound that seems entirely inappropriate. Is such a heating system really necessary in mild southern England?

Now for details. The sanctuary has a black-and-white marble pavement and, together with the proud reredos and lacy communion rail, provides a resplendent setting for the altar. The ceiling here is coved and has a central oval in a rectangle, a rosette in the middle, leaf scrolls in the spandrels, and borders with leaf and egg-and-dart. In the coving above the altar appears three cherubs' heads in clouds surrounding the sun, and otherwise acanthus fronds, leaf whorls and baskets of flowers. The nave ceiling is flat and has similar panels with the same decorative system, a larger outer panel whose decoration also includes guilloche, and a cornice with dentils, etc. Below occurs another cornice which rests upon giant panelled Corinthian pilasters, and the space between each cornice is filled with open and closed books and mitres, an unusual device. Cornices and pilasters are painted a light pink tending towards coffee, and the panelled walls are white. The chancel walls and ceilings are a light grey which appears to turn green when viewed from certain angles. Chancel and tower arches are identical. They have panelled soffits and responds, plain keystones, and heavy, block-like abaci. Above the chancel arch are two gorgeous leaf brackets. In spite of all this profuseness, the church will be remembered mainly for the Wright monument, with its dramatic gesticulating figures engaged in a frozen, yet eternal, conversation.

Box pews: Of c1728, as are all the following; plain panelling; curved corners to each block.
Chancel panelling: Plain; the westernmost sections with a bench.
Communion rail: Wrought-iron; three sided but continuously curved; vertical motifs with leaf and other scrolls.
Communion table: With plain cabriole legs.
Font: A fluted octagonal pillar; wood.
Font cover: A small, wooden, dish-shaped lid with a ball finial.
Pulpit (with tester): A two-decker; the pulpit has panels with wavy tops, the west with inlay work; panelled angle pilasters; ogee support on a fluted stem; curving stairs with thin balusters and a fluted newel; panelled back-post; large tester with rich leaf frieze and an inlay sun.
Reredos: Wide broken segmental pediment on paired Corinthian columns; outer Corinthian pilasters; pediment and entablature with enriched modillions and dentils; text boards round-arched and with enriched borders; Ten Commandments in centre, Creed on left, Lord's Prayer on right.
Royal Arms: Of George II; carved in the round. Also four hatchments.

Gayhurst: *Pulpit*

Tushingham (Old Church)

Tushingham old church lies beyond gently folded fields, concealed from the unknowing, safe in its pastoral solitude. To reach it one follows a muddy track that, unpromising at first, turns a sharp left-handed corner, then rises easily in a hedgerowed channel to a gate. At the gate a broad field opens out, a natural forecourt to the church which appears as if it were a set-piece for a Dutch landscape. Red brick amongst a mosaic

Exterior from the south-west

Interior looking east

of greens, dark coniferous forms in the churchyard, drifting shadows from cumulous clouds, piebald cattle; all remind one of Gerard Manley Hopkins' 'dappled things' and 'couple-colour'.

The church, unlike its Victorian roadside successor, stands open, welcoming and patently cared for. It was built in 1689-91, presumably in replacement of a medieval predecessor, and paid for by donation. The principal benefactor was one John Dod, a London mercer. The brickwork is of a wonderful orange-red hue, effectively contrasted against the blue-slated roof and the whole building is in a gratifying pristine condition. The plan is simple; a half-built-in west tower and a single-celled nave and chancel whose sole extension is a little projecting vestry looking as if it were a south-west transept in miniature. This lopsided facade, with the tower's west wall continued flush into what transpires to be an annexe to the vestry, is at once unexpected and amusing. The pyramid roof sets the seal upon this mark of distinction.

Of unashamedly domestic character and stylistic neutrality, the windows in the side walls are small wooden-framed and leaded facsimiles from the country cottage. Those in the chancel's east wall, two plain round-arched lights, remind one instead of the Romanesque rather than the late seventeenth century. The tower bell-openings are pairs of unadorned openings with the appearance of having been cut out of the walls. Articulation of the wall surfaces is hardly attempted and is made manifest only in the shape of plain sloping buttresses and in the segmental tympana above some windows and the doorway. Finally, the ball finials on gable ends and apexes should not be overlooked.

Inside, two features remain memorable. They are the enriched roof trusses and the carpet of straw. The impact made by the former is immediate and stunning and the experience is unique in England. Coming in through that reasonable, in-articulate doorway one is totally unprepared for this egotistical display of filigree work and the eye is constantly drawn back to them even after the initial response has subsided. The effect is attained by the employment of a single motif, a diagonally-set star impaled upon a concave-sided lozenge, repeated *ad lib*. Yet this first analysis does not exhaust the possibilities inherent in the pattern because, looked at in another way, the lozenges become bands of circles with the stars filling the spandrels. Whose was this remarkable conception? The transparent apportioning of space, the vistas through and up, are almost worthy of Bristol Cathedral's choir. One thing is certain; the designer was essentially backward-looking. The forms are Jacobean in feeling and have little to do with the end of the seventeenth century.

The placing of straws upon the floor to serve as covering must have been almost universal at one time, at least as far as country cottages, with their earthen floors, go. To find the custom still extant in this remote Cheshire church is, needless to say, most satisfying. The straw is probably swept up twice yearly and replaced by a new load. A pleasing rural aroma thus permeates the interior, a welcome change from the polish of so many churches. The straw complements to perfection the brick flooring, the homely rusticity of the benches and the clean white roof and cream walls. Only the glass in the east window wears an alien aspect; can it not be removed?

On leaving the church do not close the door without paying special attention to the door-knocker in the form of a lion's head. Being so small it will be all too easily passed by or, at most, given a superficial glance by the visitor eager to inspect the interior. Yet, in its less grandiose setting, it is as forceful as the famous Durham knocker. Its introduction has been

The roof trusses

deliberately left to the end because it seems to sum up and enshrine the cheerful friendliness of Tushingham.

Benches: Very simple; ends with three-quarter circle heads; seats and a back bar.

Benefaction Board: Commemorating the rebuilding of 1689; a cherub at the top.

Communion Table: Turned legs; band of guilloche.

Family pews: A pair flanking the altar; simple; that on the south side with knobs.

Font: An elaborately carved baluster of dark wood; gadrooned bowl; leaf decoration.

Font cover: A small lid with ribs.

Pulpit: A three-decker; panels have moulded frames; large scrolly brackets support the book-rest.

Screen: Only shoulder-high; balustrade of flat dumb-bell balusters.

West gallery: Approached up an outside staircase; two leafy brackets; in the centre panel is a re-set medieval roof boss. All furnishings are of 1689-91.

Dale

Dale is an enigmatic church. As the visitor walks down the lane past the houses of the village he will see nothing before him but a house, partly-timber-framed, partly of stone. There is also a variety of gables and cross-gables set against a sublime rising backcloth of woods. On approaching a little closer, the realization dawns that this house stands in a graveyard and that its elevations are not quite what one expects those of a house to be. In effect, only the west part, with its timber-framed upper storey, forms the house, for the rest, improbable though it may seem, represents the parish church of Dale.

How did this unique amalgam of the ecclesiastical and the secular come about? The building was, in fact, the infirmary chapel of the Premonstratensian Dale Abbey, although it only served this purpose after about 1480. Before then it had been a chantry chapel with priest's house attached, a combination which still survives elsewhere in England (eg, East Hendred, Berkshire). The Premonstratensians arrived in 1197 in replacement of a small Augustinian priory which had established itself at Dale about 1149-57. The former order was granted the site only on condition that a chantry for a member of the de Grendon family would be established nearby. Thus, Dale never was a parish church during the Middle Ages and became one only after the dissolution of the monasteries. The architectural character of the church is, therefore, entirely determined by this singular medieval background, but the interior is sheer delight to those appreciative of the post-Reformation era's furnishing activities.

The earliest external feature is the north doorway, round-arched and with a continuous chamfer. That will be about 1200, ie, shortly after the arrival of the Premonstratensians. The present ground plan is probably theirs, although the Augustinians had a church here, it seems. The chancel north and east windows are insertions of the early fourteenth century. The east window is of three lights with inset cusped ogee tracery, the north window of two lights but otherwise identical. Neither is in its original condition, but when were changes made? The local guide says about 1480 when the church was heightened and given its upper storey. Yet the surrounds look oddly unmedieval and the lights have solid stone infilling at the foot. So perhaps the windows were rebuilt during the seventeenth century in connection with the provisions of box pews, etc. However, their heads may well have been cut down when the late medieval alterations took place. These included providing nave and south aisle with a higher cross-roof, and raising the chancel roof and inserting an upper floor. That leaves only the south aisle windows which, in their present form at least, belong to the seventeenth century. They are just plain, narrow, straight-headed lights with metal casements.

The interior is a wonderful jumble of woodwork. Box pews and benches, seemingly assembled at random, crowd into every available space, and overhead hangs the boarded ceiling with its rafters and cross-beams. It is difficult to sort out where nave, chancel and aisle begin and end. In fact, architectural divisions are absent; instead there are beams and posts and braces everywhere. The chancel roof is canted and ceiled, whereas those of the nave and aisle are flat and have their rafters exposed. The upper room possesses a gallery open to the

Exterior from north-east

chancel. This is accessible from the 'infirmary', but can also be approached via a disused-looking outside staircase at the rear. The walls are roughly whitewashed and the floors partly boarded, partly of brick, ie, everything is of the utmost informality. Pulpit and reader's deck are placed behind the altar, a unique arrangement but one due, no doubt, to the confined space. Confined it most certainly is; there is hardly room to move in this most happy of 'prayer-book' interiors. Even the altar has to made do with an odd corner among the pews.

Font: C14; octagonal; the bowl with the Crucifixion, the Virgin, and shields.
Benches: c1480(?); plain straight-topped ends.
Screens: c1480(?); plain lights; plain lower panels with moulded frames.
Box pews: c1634; plain.
Communion table: c1634; boxed in during the C18.
Family pew: c1634; plain.
Pulpit: 1634; a three-decker; plain panelling; top band of upright leaf; book-rest on elegant brackets and modillions; reader's and clerk's desks with plain panelling.

Interior looking north-east

Dale: *South aisle looking west*

Parracombe (Old Church)

Parracombe church represents the epitome of building with local materials. It is as natural an element in the landscape as the rough hills all around or the rocks in that famous valley beyond Lynton. Long and low, sturdy and entirely befitting its surroundings, the church fits snugly into the flank of the high ground that, sweeping by in a wide horse-shoe, shapes the combe from which the village derives its name. With its dark stone and rugged carving and its tower kept below the brow, the church possesses the appearance of a great rock levelled and sculpted by salt-laden sea winds. No modern machine-made building could ever hope to emulate this ancient structure's craftsmanly sensibilities.

The churchyard is compact and cottagey, surrounded by thick hedges, filled with uncut grass and wild flowers, sheltered and pleasant to linger in. A low slated cottage on the south turns a rear wall towards the church while on the north side trees provide a backcloth. Beyond, a copse spreads comfortably, lively with the bustle of rooks. The tower is a four-square bastion of keep-like massiveness; perhaps it was built with defence in mind but one should remember the intractability of West Country rock. The structure is late twelfth century or possibly early thirteenth century, the oldest part of the church, and has simple round-headed windows. Each stage is divided by a string-course. The parapet, with its battlements and heavy pinnacles, is fifteenth century, as is the embattled stretch of wall between the tower and south aisle roof. After the tower comes the chancel, fully thirteenth century now, as the east window with its two plain lights indicates. The rest is all Perpendicular, ie, early sixteenth century judging by the south aisle windows with their plain round-arched lights under straight hood-moulds. The east window of this aisle has, instead, a four-centred arch, cusped lights and panel tracery; it does not necessarily point to an earlier date. The porch, part of this rebuilding campaign, has a doorway whose jambs lean at an incredible angle! Post-reformation activity was limited to the insertion of one straight-headed 'Gothic Survival' window in the nave north wall. The plain lights without arch-heads confirm the date.

If the exterior of Parracombe church is not specially individualistic, being of a type familiar in many parts of the south-west, the interior remains unique in Devon and Cornwall. It is, indeed, impeccable in its unrestored state, quite spacious and with an air of suspended decay. The Redundant Churches Fund has preserved to perfection this sense of time frozen, despite the necessary reconstruction of the roofs and other structural repairs. Yet the building is no museum piece but a living entity busy with the to-and-fro of visitors, its door forever open. Parracombe church was the first in the whole of England to be recommended for preservation by the Advisory Board for Redundant Churches. During the course of this book the reader will meet others now maintained by the Fund, none more lovable than Parracombe, but all, in their pristine condition, so sensitively cared for by this most indispensable of organisations.

The oldest architectural feature is the tower arch, shapeless, but the preamble to the most dramatic part of the interior. For the tower is open to the top, a most impressive sight with those

Exterior from the south-east

mighty walls punctuated by light accentuating the rough-and-ready stonework of the window reveals. The south arcade is typical West Country Perpendicular. The four-centred arches are characteristically moulded, the piers are of the four-shafts-and-four-hollows type and the lozenge shaped 'Devon' capitals have continuous leaf trails. Also pre-eminent in this region are the ceiled wagon roofs of the nave and aisle with leaf bosses at the intersection of ribs. The chancel roof, however, is canted and plainly plastered; its hidden timbers may well go back to the thirteenth century. Walls and roof are painted white, an effective neutral background to the furnishings. Under one's feet an old floor of buff stones undulates between the pews and then rises markedly towards the chancel.

The furnishings display a medley of browns from the red tints of the pulpit to the ochre hues of the reader's desk and adjacent family pew. Colour contrast is provided by the royal arms and other motifs on the tympanum and by the blue field on the tester. Although the furnishings are arranged in an orderly fashion their variety of line and texture guards against formality. At the west end box pews rise theatrically, their curving up sides creating an interesting wave-like motion. But the most moving aspect of the interior is the chancel, closely guarded by screen and tympanum. The old ledger stones, the raised, rough-hewn slab of the sanctuary, the simplicity of communion rail and table, the crosses and the flowers, form an ensemble full of meaning. Here the worship of centuries, the loving care of generations is synthesized and enshrined for us and the future. Redundant — never!

Font: C12; plain circular bowl; the stem must be later.
Screen: Early C15; one-light divisions; inset ogee arches with crockets and tracery.

The sanctuary

Interior looking south-west

Benches: C16; rough and plain; straight-topped ends.

Tympanum: Late C16; crowded with inscriptions; Royal Arms of George II (repainted 1758) top centre; Ten Commandments bottom centre; Lord's Prayer left; The Creed right.

Pulpit (with tester): Early C17; with plain panels and a top band of simple decoration; separate tester with the sun on a blue ground.

Texts: C17; two biblical texts in oval medallions.

Box pews: C18; plain panelling; raised in three tiers across west end; these were for musicians, etc.

Communion rail: Early C19; three-sided; square balusters with inset Gothic trefoiled arches.

Family pew: Early C19; plain panelling; the corners raised concavely.

Hat pegs: Early C19.

Reader's desk & clerk's desk: Early C19; details as family pew.

Chalbury

A humble village church standing upon the crest of a hill which presents wide views over the Dorset landscape. The building is accompanied by a rock-faced 'bungalow' to the south and a white villa, half-concealed behind a hedge, to the north. Two splendid broadly spreading beech trees effectively contrasted against the clean-limbed, white-washed simplicity of the church, introduce a strong vertical counter-emphasis to a scene that displays a predominantly horizontal flow of form. This horizontality begins with the long and narrow churchyard, is amplified by the church and bungalow and culminates in the extended horizons. Down in the valley to the east lies Horton Tower, that gigantic brick folly, ruinous now and exhibiting few reminders of the landed pride that was its *raison d'etre*.

The church, however, product of a less ostentatious tradition, enjoys a state of immaculate good health and is thoroughly approachable. Its exterior wears a Georgian coat that conceals a much longer history, for nave and chancel go back at least to the thirteenth century. The building consists of a nave with bell-turret and south porch, a chancel and a north vestry. An old drawing reproduced in the church guide depicts a tower; this must have become ruinous and perhaps financial hardship prevented the erection of a replacement, hence the bell-turret. Only a blocked lancet in the north wall of the chancel reminds us of the church's thirteenth-century origins. The east window is early fourteenth century, the date confirmed by the slight ogee tips to the trefoiled lights. In the north wall of the nave can be seen two Perpendicular windows and they survive in a hybrid half-classical state with all their tracery taken out, the resultant wide space being filled with clear glass. The process reached fruition in the remaining windows which are all eighteenth-century replacements of medieval predecessors. They are round-arched, unadorned and contain clear glass arranged in leaded rectangular panels. The porch doorway is of the same character. This Georgianizing of a medieval church occurs in other places too, eg Wasing in Berkshire. The rendered walls are scored in imitation of ashlar; the roofs are of red tiles.

The interior is small of scale and cosy, eminently characteristic in its details of the 'prayer-book' age, with an effect of orderliness and clarity. The roofs are ceiled but the tie-beams remain exposed, the neat box pews leave room for an adequate aisle and the gallery possesses its own skylight. A mild colour scheme dominated by coffee furnishings and white walls, warmed by the reds of carpet and altar cloth, provides an appropriate backcloth. Much of the embroidery is of local provenance and there exists everywhere good lettering on notices, proof of continuing faith in the buildings' validity. The electric heaters and the somewhat metallic lampshades, however, are out of place in this essentially period ensemble. Cannot more suitable fittings be installed? Interest in the furnishings is directed mainly towards the screen, for it is unique among the churches in this book. It is of the veranda type and doubles as a chancel arch. The side portions of this essentially 'Venetian window' design contain pews for squire and clergy.

Chalbury is a precious survival in the Dorset countryside, easy-going yet individualistic, a church that will rapidly earn itself a place in the affections of those who visit it.

The veranda screen

Interior looking west

Box pews: C18, as are all the following; plain panels.
Communion table: Turned legs of bulbous outline.
Family pew: Like a theatre box; broad segmental arch;
balusters along the front.
Font: A stone baluster, like a garden ornament.
Pulpit: A three-decker; plain panels.

Screen: Tripartite; veranda type; segmentally-arched
centre on four thin Tuscan columns; side parts with pew.
West gallery: Plain panels.
Communion rail: Given in 1973 in memory of Sir Owen
Morshead by the Dorset Historic Churches Trust; in the
style of c1700.

Easton (St George Reforne)

In its setting and in the character of its architecture, St George Reforne is unlike any other English church. There it stands, right on the top of Portland, like a ship at anchor among a harbour full of boats. All around lie the fragmented rocks of abandoned quarries, that strange lunar landscape from which Wren cut the stone for his cathedral and City churches. Here, the walls of the church and the innumerable gravestones

Interior looking east

exposed to the full force of the wind create an immense three-dimensional advertisement for the durability of Portland stone. The strange whiteness of this stone against a crisp blue sky, the rich green textures of the tangled grass, the endless rows of often bizarre-shaped memorials and the haunting loneliness of the site leave a dream-like impression on the mind of an almost surrealist intensity. Few other churches in the whole of England can exert such an emphatic presence upon the landscape and yet appear also as a logical extension of the rocks beneath.

St George Reforne, speaking in ecclesiastical terms, is one of the foremost examples, outside London, of that style known as English Baroque, the style created in the Office of Works just before 1700 and developed by Vanbrugh, Hawksmoor and Archer. In terms of chronological development, the building comes very near the end of this somewhat short-lived phase in our architectural history. It was begun in 1754 and completed only in 1766, ie, long after the major architects had turned, or been converted, to Palladianism. Wren died in 1723, Vanbrugh in 1726 and Hawksmoor in 1736; yet St George Reforne owes something to all three. It was designed by Thomas Gilbert, a local man, and he looked to Wren, rather than Gibbs who was generally more influential in the provinces, for his plan and spire arrangement. From Vanbrugh and Hawksmoor come most of the details. Yet the church is not in the least derivative or provincial; Gilbert must have enjoyed a true rapport with the Baroque and exploits its felicities boldly and convincingly.

The church consists of a sturdy west tower, a long nave, broad and shallow transepts and a short apsed chancel. At the crossing of nave and transepts the internal dome is covered by a kind of truncated circular 'pyramid', perhaps the only unsatisfactory detail of the design. It will be observed that the transepts project equidistantly and the resulting centralizing plan is certainly of Wren derivation. The windows are arranged in two tiers, tall and round-arched above, short and segmental-arched below. Their unenriched raised frames are typical of Vanbrugh and Hawksmoor. The windows are sashed, a curiously secular touch. A lunette occupies the space within each transept pediment. These facades remind one of Archer's Aynho Park in Northamptonshire. The blank niches and roundels in the apse are balanced by similar motifs in the ground stage of the tower. The latter is the highwater mark of the composition and has a striking bell-stage consisting of a square chore with aedicules (ie, openings framed by columns and entablature) carrying urns. The concave sides of the top stage are reminiscent of Archer though the ensemble again reminds one of Wren. If there exists a fault in the design of the church it is perhaps this. The heavy turret-like projections at each end of the nave seem to imply a termination, a containment of those parts which lie between. They also demand proper east and west facades. Yet the eye is forced to travel on, eastwards to the apse, westwards to the tower. The latter thus become liturgical afterthoughts, secondary limbs attached to an essentially secular and symmetrical body.

The interior is spacious and formal, ably restored to its original condition by the Redundant Churches Fund after years of disgusting neglect. Despite the presence of three galleries, a full set of box pews and the twin pulpits, the width and height of the building negate any sense of overcrowding. Articulation of the wall surfaces is kept to a minimum. Only the east window displays an enrichment of its surround; its Tuscan pilasters supporting sections of entablature are repeated in the chancel arch and also, but set parallel to the wall plane, in the arch differentiating chancel and apse. The cornice, segmental plaster vaults and the shallow saucer-dome are completely plain. It is a cool, somewhat clinical interior, an impression reinforced by the colour scheme of beige and grey. What makes it memorable and especially telling amongst 'prayer-book' interiors are two things. Firstly, those pews lying between pulpit and altar have their seats facing west, ie,

The twin pulpit and reader's desk

away from the ritual focus of Christian worship! It is a remarkable survival, the only extant instance of this extreme low-church arrangement. How it survived fifty years of Tractarian upheaval is a mystery. Secondly, we have the identical pulpit and reader's desk nodding to each other across the gangway. They form the focal point, both visually and liturgically, of the church, with the pews gathered around them. Such twin pulpits also occur at, eg, Mildenhall in Wiltshire, and in two or three other churches, but never with the visual force displayed here.

St George Reforne was replaced by a new church in 1917. From then on the story was a downhill one, from disuse, through neglect, to misuse and dereliction. Then, in 1968, a group of Friends was formed to save it and their work culminated in the church being vested in the Redundant Churches Fund in 1971. Now St George Reforne stands triumphantly whole again, its future as Portland's architectural centrepiece assured.

Communal rail: C17; with vertically-symmetrical turned balusters.
Baptismal pew: c1760, as are all the following; seats arranged around the font.
Box pews: Tall narrow panels; numbered.
Clerk's pew: Behind the pulpit; small.
Font: A bulbous stone baluster.
Galleries: Three; on thin columns; simple panelling.
Pulpit & Reader's desk: Identical; stilted blank arches on strong Tuscan pilasters; slim octagonal stems; curving metal stairs.
Rector's & Squire's pews: As box pews but with raised backs; they face west, of course.
Communion table: Modern? It does not appear in pre-restoration photographs.

Leweston

The first impression of Leweston church and house is a disappointing one. Both buildings, as one approaches from the north, appear together as a sombre rendered group set against the light of a southward sky. But once in the forecourt of the house the pair separate visually and the external beauties of the church become apparent. It is a beauty composed of several facets; the general proportions and character of the building,

Interior looking east

the sense of craftsmanship explicit in every detail and the warm panoply of colour. It is the latter which one responds to in the first instance, the rich brown stone of windows sharply contrasted against the buff of rendered walls and backed by the deep greens of a splendid cedar. Another even more magnificent cedar, far larger than the church, occupies one corner of the churchyard. The latter, with its neat lawns and herbaceous borders, retains the character of a garden and, indeed, flows easily and naturally into the real garden of the house.

Leweston church is an important example of a small chapel erected by a landowner for the use of his household. It was built in 1616 by Sir John Fitzjames and remains absolutely in its original condition. Although having the appearance of a small private chapel it has on several separate occasions been accorded the status of a parish church. Now, together with the house, it belongs to a private convent school and is no longer owned by the Anglican church. A mass is occasionally sung but regular services take place in the modern chapel opposite. Despite such infrequent use this charming little building is maintained in an excellent state of preservation.

It consists of a single nave-cum-chancel, only two bays in length, with a lovely stone bellcote perched upon the west gable, and a lower west porch. This is entered from the south and is distinguished by a lunette with a ball finial. With the exception of this lunette and some low-key strapwork on the bellcote, the details are entirely Gothic Survival, ie 'debased' Perpendicular, though one should perhaps avoid this derogatory term so confidently employed by the Victorians. The windows are composed of three uncusped arched lights, the centre raised and set under a stepped-up hood-mould. This arrangement occurs in several other Dorset churches hereabouts (Minterne Magna of about 1615-20, Ryme Intrinsica and Folke of 1628) and forms an interesting local 'school'. That this school or workshop was operating in a Survival manner is confirmed by the essentially Late Perpendicular forms. The whole question of Survival versus Revival, however, will be discussed in greater detail when describing Staunton Harold. The east window, with its plain panel tracery is, indeed, very close to Perpendicular precedent, and the doorway possesses a typical 'Tudor' arch. Fitzjames' coat of arms is displayed above, under yet another stepped-up hood-mould.

Upon entering, one will not fail to notice the two huge clock weights suspended from pulleys above their own well, and the heavy 'thunk thunk' emanating from the mechanism relentlessly accompanies the visitor's exploration of the church. The interior holds few special surprises except that it appears unexpectedly lofty with the pointed barrel roof floating high overhead. Interest is concentrated in the furnishings. They are amazingly well preserved; the benches with their ends of an uncanny human countenance, the wall panelling, the altar and the two-decker pulpit fitting neatly into the corner, as they were in Fitzjames' time. The style is Jacobean, not Gothic, since although applied design had turned Renaissance via France and the Low Countries, architecture had no other exemplar but that of the medieval past. Leweston is the best preserved example of a Jacobean church built and furnished in one operation; only Langley in Shropshire can approach it in authenticity.

Throughout the Middle Ages the Roman Catholic church was the universal patron of all that was best in art and architecture. It is sad therefore, to find here the inevitable mass-produced angels and collecting boxes. Surely something more appropriate could be installed, possibly made by the

The clock weights

school's pupils or by a local craftsman.

Font: C13; circular; plain.
Benches: c1616, as are all the following; ends with rounded tops and roundels; shallow leaf and strapwork decoration.
Communion table: With fluted pilasters and strapwork.
Pulpit (with tester): A two-decker; pilasters with arabesque; much decoration in high relief; broad angled back panel with fishes; tester with knob pendants and egg-and-dart.
Reredos: Really a raised continuation of the panelling; three Ionic pilasters, two fluted, one with arabesque; a rose and thistle above.
Wall panelling: Pilasters with arabesque; plain panelling.

Winterborne Tomson

Exterior from the south-east

This tiny church, one of the architectural gems of Dorset and of England, too, stands amongst farm buildings in the shallow valley of the Winterborne Brook. It is accompanied by a thatched cottage, behind which it hides, an ugly modernized farmyard to the north, and over to the east behind trees, the much larger farmhouse. If it were not for these trees and a few more around the cottage, the setting would appear austere indeed. For the church itself is exceptionally severe in its outline and the churchyard concurs. In fact, the latter must number amongst the barest in the country for it consists of a simple square enclosure containing just one decrepit tomb and otherwise cropped grass. Yet the wonderful medley of colour in the walls, helped along by lichen patches, provides warm relief. Outside occurs more cropped grass, and several mushroom-like bollards. It is a perfect environment for this lowly church; anything more elaborate or assertive would detract from the building's poignancy.

Winterborne Tomson is one of only four Norman single-celled apsidal churches in England (Nately Scures in Hampshire is another), the only later addition being a little weatherboarded bell-turret. The walls are an haphazard mixture of flint and greyish stone and the roof, continuous over nave and apse, is of red tiles. The precise date is almost impossible to ascertain; the apse suggests early rather than later Norman but the one remaining window does not help much. That the bell-turret could be eighteenth or nineteenth century does not matter either; it is wrong to approach this church in such a date-hunting spirit. It is enough to know that its character is governed by its Norman parentage; Early English, Decorated or Perpendicular architects would have produced a different interpretation. Be that as it may, the windows which range along the south wall are, indeed, the late Middle Ages' answer to the problem of providing sufficient illumination. Their paired, uncusped arched lights under straight hood-moulds indicate an early sixteenth-century date. The purist would argue that they negate the essential Normanness of the church but they do make for a more honest witness to countless generations of worshippers. The featureless west doorway, with its massive studded door, is probably later.

The interior is marvellous, just a single room covered by a ceiled wagon roof (early sixteenth century no doubt) that flows easily into the apse where its ribs are set radially. The sole enrichment are the leaf bosses at the intersections of the ribs. In fact, these bosses represent the only attempt at decoration for the furnishings are quietly unpretentious. Yet they are so perfectly apt; it is incredible to think that six hundred years separate their installation from the church's erection. What job would the Victorians have made of re-equipping such an interior? Pitch pine and hard Gothic trim? Could we today produce as satisfying an ensemble out of modern materials? We might, knowing that our aesthetic sensibilities towards the historic past have evolved so much since the nineteenth century and that we are no longer blinded by arrogant self-righteousness or reforming zeal. The furnishings date from about 1716-37, the years of Archbishop Wake of Canterbury, and are of a lovely scrubbed light brown. Everything is there, the west gallery all askew and reached via nothing more than a ladder, the box pews with simple hinges, the little two-decker pulpit whose tester is supported by a chain, the communion rail and table and the pews for vicar and squire. The floor is of stone flags, pitted and grooved, the walls whitewashed. The altar frontal introduces a splash of red. A restoration, just in time, took place in 1931. It was carried out at the instigation of the Society for the Protection of Ancient Buildings by A.R.

Interior looking west

Powys and money was raised by the sale of some Hardy manuscripts.

Font: C15; octagonal; plain; the top cut down.
Box pews: Of c1716-37, as are all the following; plain panelling.
Communion table: With twisted legs.
Pulpit (with tester): A two-decker; plain.
Screen: Very simple; rectangular openings.
Squire's & Vicar's pews: Flanking the altar; plain panelling.
West gallery: Plain panelling.

Interior looking east

Hailes

Exterior from the south-west

The picture presented by Hailes as the visitor approaches from the north is an almost archetypal Cotswold one. The rich golden stone of the church and its stone-slated roofs, and the wooded hills behind, could be repeated a hundred times over and beyond the scarp. Yet Hailes, to be precise, lies in front of the hills themselves and turns its face more towards the timber-framed country of Worcestershire. While the medieval builders looked naturally to the oolitic limestone nearby, later carpenters provided a bell-turret which, though in its present condition probably not older than the nineteenth century, forms a link with the black-and-white of the Marches. The church stands in a pretty, close-fitting churchyard liberally supplied with roses and overlooks broad, flat fields to the north. On the south trees provide framed views of windows and walling. Only the too formal shape of an adjacent carpark (gravel, not tarmac, thank goodness) detracts somewhat from this unspoiled *tableau vivant*.

Hailes church consists of a nave with bell-turret and south porch, and a lower chancel. The roofs are quite steep, a feature that, where original, generally points to a pre-Perpendicular date. A small sanctus bellcote, hardly attempting to compete with the bell-turret for attention, perches upon the nave's eastern gable. The bell-turret has wooden louvres and a pyramid roof. Could it be as recent as 1905, the date of the innocuous porch? The date of the church itself has not yet been established. If the Transitional chancel arch represents the original phase, it is late twelfth century. The exterior, however, betrays nothing of this, except for the buttresses on the south side which may be contemporary, for all windows were replaced during the early fourteenth century. Of these windows, those in the chancel north wall (and one opposite) are the most interesting. Each light has below its plainly-arched head an inset cinquecusped ogee with a trefoil in the spandrel. The three-light east window displays, instead, cusped reticulated tracery, that characteristic motif of the Decorated style. Also not to be overlooked are the ogee tips to the trefoiled heads of the nave west window. One further window, that to the left of the porch, deserves a mention. Here the trefoiled head is repeated in depth, resulting in a double-layered profile.

So much for the exterior; now inside. The interior effect is one of uncluttered simplicity. In that, it echoes the exterior and, although the furnishings are not typically 'prayer-book', at least in the nave, the overall impression is an unrestored one. Instead of box pews ranged along each side, we have plain pre-Reformation benches overtopped by a pulpit that is neither a two or three-decker. Admittedly, there is a box pew in the north-west corner but this may have served as a baptismal pew. Yet if that is the case, was another font not kept here, or has the medieval one been moved to its present position more recently? As an effective contrast to the liturgical neutrality met with up to this point, the chancel presents an ensemble that is rigidly Puritan in its arrangement. For here the communion table stands not against the east wall but centrally and is surrounded on three sides by a bench seat affixed to the stalls. Only Langley in Shropshire preserves something similar, although there the table is placed broadside in front of a west-facing communion rail-cum-bench. At Hailes a point of confusion arises; there are two communion tables. The answer is that the altar is the original seventeenth-century one and the other a recent introduction brought in, no doubt, to restore the

The chancel furnishings

Puritan disposition. It is regrettable that present-day Anglican liturgy requires an eastern altar, thus betraying the authenticity of this rare survival. Yet no church can be a museum.

We have said nothing yet about the architectural features of the interior, the tiles, or the wall paintings. The chancel arch is, at first sight, late twelfth century. The responds have one demi-shaft and one nook-shaft carrying old worn multi-scallop capitals, and the pointed arch has two rolls. Now, this combination of a pointed arch and the aforementioned capitals points to a date of about 1180. Yet the arch itself may be a later alteration, in which case the date of the responds, and of the church, can be pushed back to about 1130. The roofs of nave and chancel, the former single-framed and with tie-beams, kingposts and two-way struts, the latter with exposed timber-framing between the wall plates, are probably fourteenth century. Too little can be said here concerning the extremely interesting series of wall paintings in both nave and chancel; the faded St Christopher that greets the visitor as he enters possesses a strange ghost-like aspect that is not a little disquieting. The tiles come from Hailes Abbey; they are collected mainly in the chancel. A pleasantly uneven set of stone flags forms the floor of the nave. Altogether, Hailes preserves an enjoyable interior of varying stylistic mood and character and forms a fitting companion to the more unified Little Washbourne further along the road.

Font: C13; octagonal; plain.
Tiles: C13, etc; in the chancel and by the south door; shields, etc; predominantly red and yellow.
Wall paintings: Early C14; St Cecilia and St Margaret in niches; dragons and other mythical beasts in spandrels above windows; coats of arms in square panels; upper frieze of standing figures under foiled canopies (chancel); large St Christopher; a hunting scene (nave).
Benches: C15 or early C16; plain straight-topped ends.
Screen: C15; one-light divisions with inset cusped ogee tracery, repeated below; upper and lower vine trails.
Stained glass: C15; nine Apostles; mainly yellow and white.
Box pews: C17; plain panelling; top band of enrichment; good hinges.
Communion table: Mid C17; turned legs.
Stalls: Mid C17; arranged two-deep around communion table; front bench on turned legs; plain panelling.
Wall panelling: Mid C17; plain.
Pulpit (with tester): C18; large and square; plain.

Box pew door hinge

Little Washbourne

Interior looking west

The time to visit Little Washbourne is in high summer. Then, the already secluded church becomes a veritable recluse introspectively concealed within a web of vegetation. The churchyard disappears beneath a shoulder-high growth of grasses, nettles and hedge parsley, while over everything, even the mangled trees of a decaying orchard, goosegrass climbs in all directions. Yet the churchyard should not be considered neglected or desecrated; rather the reverse, in fact. For here the visitor can revel in Nature joyously unfettered, no longer constricted by the too often insensitive hand of Man. What has become inconvenient and outmoded for one species now provides an undisturbed habitat for others less ambitious in their territorial demands.

The church is outwardly austere, yet rugged and fortress-like, with mighty battered buttresses enhancing the already dependable walls. The impression is one of clear rectangles and diagonals, of unchanging plastic forms, contrasted against the constantly evolving filamentous vegetation. Nave and chancel are basically twelfth century, though few details remain. The west wall still preserves its trio of flat, pilaster-like buttresses and a string-course, and the chancel north window, a tiny round-arched light with deep internal reveals, immediately proclaims its Norman parentage. As for those features not lost, it can be assumed that most survived until the Georgian rehabilitation. Those telling signs of later medieval development, such as blocked arch-heads, etc, do not occur anywhere and it is logical to look upon the present windows as late eighteenth-century enlargements of Norman predecessors. So the external character now is more 'churchwarden' than medieval.

These post-medieval features, to say it again, are of the late eighteenth century, the date confirmed by the windows with their broad pointed arches and by the Y-tracery battening of the door. They impart a slight Gothick character. In retrospect, it is the buttresses, those giant set-squares forming powerful diagonal rhythms, which remain in the memory. Those against the chancel east wall, with the window set between, create a monumental group. They are indicative of an urgent need for repair at that time. The prominent bell-turret belongs to this campaign, also, although the timber structure inside points to medieval ancestry. It has rendered walls, horizontal louvre bands and a pyramid roof. Finally, the lantern above the doorway provides a pleasant homely and period touch.

The interior is clean and orderly, very even-toned and enriched by the high quality of the furnishings. Only the unwelcome cracks in the plaster detract, yet even they create interesting abstract patterns around the chancel arch. The floor is stone flagged, as usual, and very regular. Box pews and pulpit display a reddish tinge and their deeply-sculptured panels are highlighted by an ample flood of light from the clear glass in its leaded framework. The chancel arch is Norman and fairly inarticulate. It has nook-shafts carrying multi-scallop capitals and plain responds, arch and abaci. What is the date of the roofs? Fourteenth century? They have plain tie-beams and rafters but the bell-turret timbers, partly boarded in, include a braced collar truss. The lighting is by candles on tall moveable standards that form an avenue along the nave. It is a system entirely appropriate to the setting and one is thankful for the absence of junction boxes and cables clamped to the walls. Would that more churches were satisfied with this humble kind of lighting. Little Washbourne is maintained by the Redundant Churches Fund.

Box pews: Late C18, as are all the following; deep panelling with inturned corners.

Communion rail: Plain square balusters.

Communion table: An elaborate piece with a marble top; square tapering legs; four diagonal base ties of ogee shape with pierced quarterfoils.

Pews: Open pews raised theatrically at the west end.

Pulpit (with tester): A two-decker; panelling with inturned corners and inlay work; tester with dentils and inlay.

Font: C19 (?); octagonal; cusped ogee tracery; angle shafts on corbels.

The tester

Avington

The position is secluded, yet immediately accessible. The churchyard gateway provides a 'window' in a framework of brick-and-flint walling. From anywhere else in the single-street village the church remains tantalizingly concealed from view. Inside the gate, a trail of stepping stones beckons the visitor forwards between more walls and guides his feet up to the door. The churchyard is a perfect complement to the

staleness of the church. It is exceptionally well looked after and, with its impeccable lawns, shrubs, roses, flower beds and trees, evokes the atmosphere of a private garden. Yet, this tells only half the story, for the churchyard is divided, literally, into two unconnected sections by walls abutting against tower and chancel. To gain access to the north part, one must go through the church and out by the north door, the aristocrat's entrance. Here, all is unkempt and neglected, a narrow strip of wildness left to its own devices. It comes as a shock, indeed, after the serenity of the south side. Over the wall to the south-east appears the former rectory, yellow brick for contrast, set against a screen of foliage.

Avington church was built in 1768-71. The material is brick, a lovely rich red brick with fine mortar joints. Architecturally backward in its motifs, few details point to an awareness of emerging Neo-Classicism. The designer, whoever he was, looked back through Gibbs to the early eighteenth century. The tower certainly displays something of the massiveness and forcefulness of English Baroque, and the embattled parapets especially link the design to Vanbrugh's evocation of the medieval past. The tower is of three stages divided by thin, yet prominent string-courses and has pilaster-buttresses at the angles. The west window is of Venetian type, with the centre blank, and the doorways have Gibb's surrounds. These characteristic surrounds of alternating quoins also enrich the main doorway into the church. All other windows, including those in the body of the church, are plain, keyed-in, round-arched lights. The nave windows display pretty Gothick intersecting glazing bars, and that is something fully up-to-date. Only the east wall attempts more in its articulation; the Venetian window is as in the tower, though of course larger, and above it is a keyed-in circular window under a pedimental

A certain coolness pervades the interior, though it is lovely all the same with the pink walls and blue ceiling, and the details possess just enough richness to bring everything to life. An emphasis upon curved lines can be discerned, from the barrel vaulted roof and the window arches, through the broadly bowed corners of the pews and the swept-up side panel of the pulpit stairs, to the elaborate curls of the communion rail. The plain roof has a pink central oval with an enriched leaf border and fan. The cornice is simple, and it is around the east end that major enrichment occurs. It is one of the most richly-appointed sanctuaries of any church in this book. The east window is bolection-moulded, has a band of metopes and triglyphs at the springing of the central arch, an elaborate leafy volute keystone, and the three lights are linked by more metopes. Below, the reredos displays the same ornateness, and amongst the small-scale ornamentation is a band of quarterfoils maintaining the Gothick connection. The panels with the usual texts are painted blue. In front of all this is a beautiful pavement of veined marble. Now back to the quieter nave. The windows here have demi-rolls, fluted keystones and rest upon volute brackets decorated with leaf. The tower arch reflects the central section of the east window but is much more reticent. Before leaving, attention should be directed towards the perfectly even stone floor, in places worn shiny with age, the florid chandelier and that most lovable possession of Avington church, the dear little Gothick barrel organ up on the gallery.

In toto, Avington is one of the finest medium-sized Georgian village churches in England. The faultless condition of church and churchyard is indicative of the parishioners' high regard for their architectural heritage; the large notice at the gate satisfactorily indicates their awareness of Avington's regional importance. Long may such appreciation continue.

Communion rail: detail

Box pews: 1771, as are all the following; bowed corners; plain panelling; set back around the font at west end.
Chancel panelling: Dropped concavely under the windows; plain.
Chandelier: Two tiers of branches; Baroque stem; leaf bases to candle holders.
Communion rail: Of lead(?); with groups of vertical shapes arranged in threes; much scrollwork and leaves; wooden rail with two knobs.
Communion table: Plain.
Family pew: Taller; bowed corners; plain panelling; internal panelling with enriched frames, metopes and circles.
Font: A veined marble baluster; gadrooned base.
Font cover: Circular and almost flat with just a slight dome.
Hat pegs: Two sets along the north wall.
Pulpit (with tester): A three-decker; panels with raised lunette tops; dentils; thin back-post with a fluted pilaster; tester with S-shapes, dentils and an ogee canopy with enriched ribs and a dove on top; reader's and clerk's desks with plain panelling, the latter with a bowed corner.
Reredos: Open segment pediment on fluted Corinthian columns; outer fluted Corinthian pilasters; fluted bases; entablature with metopes and triglyphs, egg-and-dart, dentils, lozenges and quarterfoils; enriched panels with Ten Commandments, Lord's Prayer and Creed.
Royal Arms: Of George III.
West Gallery: On two fluted Corinthian pilasters; deep cornice with modillions; centre brought forward and flanked by broad fluted pilasters; dentil frieze.
Barrel organ: Early C19; a charming Gothick piece; crocketed ogee gable with pierced cusping; obelisk finials. Also one hatchment.

Avington: *Interior looking west*

Minstead

This New Forest church is southern England's answer to Whitby and, like its more famous northerly cousin, presents an invitingly varied facade to the visitor. It is sufficiently different from others to arrest attention at once and demands close inspection from even the most casual, architecturally unconcerned tourist. From the lych-gate one sees a medley of cross-gables and dormers set against broad horizontal bands of red tiling, the latter those of the nave and chancel roofs. There is much white woodwork and bargeboarding, and the whole is crowned by a miniature cupola-cum-spirelet. Against this informality the churchyard appears contrived indeed, too contrived in fact; something less rigid in layout and planting would allow for an easier rapport between building and ground. This, though, is a verdict condemning the north side only, for around to the south, where the churchyard flows downwards into the surrounding landscape, rough grass and an absence of clearly-defined paths prevail. The change is patent and readily appreciated. Among the headstones are many of the eighteenth century sporting a beautiful array of lichens.

The description of the exterior must begin by docketing the components of the building. They are a west tower, a nave with north porch and north chapel, a south transept, and a chancel with north chapel and south vestry. Building materials are equally diverse; stone for the chancel, rendering for nave and transept, brick for the rest. The architectural development is also a long and complex one. It begins in the thirteenth century with the erection of a nave and chancel and possibly a west tower. What did this replace? Perhaps a wooden Saxon church, as it seems unlikely that a Norman one would have been demolished entirely after only a hundred years. Of the thirteenth century we have the north doorway with two rolls in the arch and two orders of nook-shafts. Only one further medieval feature remains, viz, the nave south window, fifteenth century and straight-headed.

The rest is all post-Reformation, a happy accumulation of insertions and extensions. We begin in the early seventeenth century with a window originally inserted into the nave south wall but removed and re-set at the end of the transept when the latter was built in 1792. Its three plain lights under a straight hood-mould are typical of the date. The porch is of 1683 and is, with its wooden segmental-arched doorway, plain bargeboards and the pendant-cum-finial, especially charming. Much work was carried out during the eighteenth century, not all of it dated. The west tower, however, was built in 1774. It is a very quiet, one might say inarticulate, structure with plain arched windows, lunette bell-openings, plain parapet with obelisk pinnacles of stone, and the previously mentioned spirelet. The wooden Y-tracery goes well with the date. The long south transept of 1792 possesses few details of note. It is simply a utilitarian extension designed to accommodate as much seating as possible and at a reasonable price. Apart from the seventeenth-century window, there exist just two others near the nave. They are wooden-framed and have inset trefoil-cusping, a Georgian interpretation of the fifteenth-century window close by. The north windows of the nave, including two dormers, are a varied trio, all wooden-

framed and domestic, as we have met them at Tushingham. This also applies to the windows of the north chapels, probably late eighteenth century too. The chancel east window is mildly Gothick; two lancet lights with cruciform abaci.

The interior is an endearing assemblage of galleries, box pews and other accessories. There is even an upper west gallery, and it is worth seeking out the key to the tower doorway in order to clamber right to the top. Up there, under the roof, one feels like the captain of a ship. Down below, the raised floor of the chancel looks suspiciously Tractarian but is of about 1790. It was raised by the Comptons to provide a family vault. The furnishings here are not what they seem. The chancel rail is of 1915, the panelling of 1921 and the communion rail is also recent, perhaps with re-used parts. Yet they are entirely acceptable, which is more than one can say for the communion table, an overtly Gothic Victorian monstrosity mercifully concealed by the altar cloth. The only really distracting feature is the wide opening into the transept. Where one expects enclosure there exists, instead, spacial amplitude. It creates a disturbing unbalance yet allows for an exquisite view into the nave. A superb cast-iron column gives support to the beam hidden behind the plastered ceiling. All roofs are ceiled, barrel-vaulted in nave and chancel, canted in the transept. A nice Puritan touch is the placing of the font before the pulpit, an arrangement condemned by the ecclesiologists. Of architectural features, there is only the double-chamfered chancel arch, thirteenth century and perhaps altered. Its two orders of shafts carry moulded capitals. The floors, where one can see them, are of red tiles.

To sum up, Minstead presents a vivid impression of a whole village community gathered together for prayers, Hardyesque in its intensity. No other church, except Whitby, can equal it.

The galleries

The nave

Font: Late C12; Purbeck marble; square bowl with tapering sides; four shafts and a circular stem; bowl with carvings (Christ with the Cross, stylized eagles, the Lamb and Cross, two lions with one head).

Benches: C17; plain ends.

Pulpit (with tester): C17; a three-decker; plain panelling; back-post with a blank arch and arabesque leaf; plain tester; much repair work with plain vertical boarding.

West & north galleries: C18; on plain chamfered posts; plain panelling, two with benefactions; north gallery raised segmentally over doorway.

Commandment boards: Late C18; in frames with pendant arches; a similar frame around the east window.

Prayer desks: Late C18; in the north-east chapel; each has a book-rest on twisted balusters.

Wall panelling: Late C18; in the same chapel; plain; painted white; also a fireplace with dentils.

Box pews: Of c1792; in a stepping-up arrangement; plain panelling; at the back C19 pitch-pine copies of the C17 benches.

Hat pegs: Also of c1792; long rows in the transept.

Wall panelling: Early C19(?); in the nave; plain vertical boarding.

Upper west gallery: Of 1818; on two thin posts; plain square balusters.

Clodock

Exterior from the south-east

Clodock is especially favoured in its setting; this south-west corner of Herefordshire is one of the most beautiful places in all England. Alternating parallel bands of wooded hills and verdant valleys run up from the intricate landscape of Monmouthshire and pay supplication to the mightiest ridge of them all, the great wall of the Black Mountains. Each valley possesses its own stream, clear and uncontaminated, and the light, that marvellous liquid light of the Welsh border, weaves its spell over everything, creating an enchanting land of serene privacy. Here one seems a world away from the visual and spiritual horrors of industrialised and motorised England. The church and its surroundings form a microcosm of the wider scene. The hand-wrought honesty of rough sandstone walls, the rushing stream deep down below the churchyard, the green panoply of woods, fields and hedgerows, and the inevitable skyline of hills, could be repeated, separately or together, a hundred times in this border country.

Clodock church is built of that red sandstone so characteristic of Herefordshire, Shropshire, etc. It is a lovely material, in both texture and colour, and the building would appear more satisfying still if it were not for the mean blue slate roofs. The original roofs were of higher pitch, as can be seen by the marks against the east side of the tower. The church consists of a west tower, a nave with south porch, and a chancel. The nave is Norman and two windows, single small round-arched lights, survive in the north wall. A rebuilding of the chancel took place at the end of the twelfth century, ie, it is Transitional, as one can see by the sole remaining lancet in the north wall. South doorway and south porch may be contemporary, judging by their single-chamfered pointed arches. The porch, though, looks interfered with, and the bargeboards could be seventeenth century or later.

Subsequent medieval alterations consist, apart from the tower, of a variety of window insertions. They begin in the late thirteenth century with the chancel east window and the south-east window in the nave. Both display that typical Herefordshire variation of the three-stepped-lights-under-one-arch theme wherein the arch of the centre light is opened out, the mullions being carried straight up to the window head. The large window in the nave, with its cusped ogee lights under a straight head, is fourteenth century and Decorated. The two remaining nave windows are fifteenth century; one has a little tracery. Also Perpendicular and late fifteenth century is the three-stage tower. This has an embattled parapet and two-light bell-openings with depressed arches. The stairs project slightly on the south side. In a church of this nature one expects to discover at least something post-Reformation and in the chancel south window we have just that. Its two plain straight-headed lights constitute a feature recognisably seventeenth century. The huge and bulky buttresses, with their vague set-offs, may be of that time too.

The interior is much more characterful. It is only inside that the forcefulness and spaciousness of the twelfth-century nave can be truly appreciated. Before entering, one does not anticipate quite such a striking room. It is so spacious, in fact, that the box pews and gallery do not overcrowd or impose themselves at all. The walls are openly massive and would appear so even if the deep reveals were not there, for the rough plastering implies a great thickness of wall behind. The late twelfth-century chancel arch speaks a different language, at

Interior looking east

once more slender and linear, evidence of the emerging Gothic style. Its arch is pointed and double-chamfered, the inner order on nook-shafts, its capitals multi-scalloped. Behind the altar is a blocked depressed arch of exceptionally plain outline. This must have led into a low vestry, unless it was erected for a burial. As part of the seventeenth (or eighteenth) century strengthening, inner responds were added to the chancel arch. They run straight up into the arch, a disquieting effect. The roofs, with their canted boarding, are probably of the restoration of 1916-9, but the tie-beams are, of course, medieval.

The box pews are a real hotchpotch, arranged in three rows, which is unusual, and with variations within each row. In age they range through the late seventeenth century. One block, adjacent to the pulpit, was removed in 1916 but to no ill effect. In the chancel, the table stands forward from the wall and is accompanied by a long bench, the housel bench, upon which the waiting communicants sat. It is the only one of its kind in our fifty churches. While the furnishings express Low Church liturgical needs, one feature vividly portrays the seventeenth and eighteenth-century attitude to the 'rude and barbaric' medieval past. Around the chancel north window occurs a painted architectural design that attempts to convert the Gothic lancet into a Classical window. It represents the same attitude, only in reverse, that allowed the nineteenth century Gothicists to insert Middle-Pointed tracery into Georgian windows.

The painted architecture around the chancel north window

Font: Late C12; plain circular bowl and stem.
Stalls: 1657 (N) & 1668 (S); with circular and obelisk finials and arabesque leaf and dragons; the front stalls on both sides are recent but appropriate.
Box pews: Late C17; plain panelling; one, centre front, with turned knobs and an arabesque frieze; one, north row west, a double pew with a door between each section.
Communion rail: Late C17; three-sided; turned balusters and knobs.
Communion table: Late C17; with turned legs.
Housel bench: Late C17; plain.
Painted texts: Late C17 & C18; Ten Commandments, Lord's Prayer and a Royal Arms; very worn.
Pulpit (with tester): Late C17; a three-decker; plain panelling; back-post with openwork leaf left and right; tester with an acanthus leaf boss.
Chest: 1695; plain.
Painted decorations: c1700; around chancel north window; pediment and finial.
West gallery: c1715; on two fluted posts; plain panelling; wide staircase in two flights with turned balusters; seat backs with short turned balusters.
Benefaction tablet: 1805; stone; plain pilasters with pineapple finials; a slightly Gothick centre with a mandorla.

Shobdon

Among the *incunabula* of the Georgian Gothic Revival, Shobdon must take pride of place. It is the *prima donna* of that frivolous Rococo Gothick popularized by William Kent, the style which was to be superseded by the more serious-minded work of Horace Walpole at Strawberry Hill. Kent began to design in the Gothick about 1730 (remodelling of the Clock Court gatehouse at Hampton Court) and went on to initiate a fashion for Gothick fireplaces, etc, which were really Classical composition overlaid with a thin veneer of pseudo-medieval detail. That, in essence, is the Kentian philosophy; the creation of a patternbook of medievalizing designs which would be understandable to those whose taste in architecture had been moulded by Palladianism. To such patrons, looking for a more Romantic idiom than the followers of Lord Burlington could provide, Kent's whimsical novelties appeared especially attractive. The style was soon labelled 'modern Gothick'. Yet Kent, it must not be forgotten, was a protegé of Burlington.

In 1748 Horace Walpole commenced Strawberry Hill and, in doing so, began to change the course of the revival. From then onwards, the translation of medieval motifs became ever more archaeological, although it was not until the reign of Queen Victoria that a true understanding manifested itself, as in the works of Pugin, Scott and the rest. Shobdon stands at this mid-Georgian crossroads. It was built in 1752-6 by the Hon Richard Bateman of Shobdon Court. The architect is unfortunately not known, but Bateman was a friend of Walpole who had converted him 'from a Chinese to a Goth'. Yet, internally at least, there is much of the Chinoiserie about Shobdon. So who did design the church? Henry Flitcroft has been suggested. He, however, had no connections with Strawberry Hill and was, in fact, a designer of Palladian buildings, being known as 'Burlington Harry'. So it is most likely that the creator of this little Gothick toy was a member of the Bateman-Walpole circle, even perhaps a member of the 'Committee' itself, such as Richard Bentley.

The west tower is basically thirteenth century, since Bateman only rebuilt a medieval church. Most details, however, are Gothick and eminently typical of the genre. The ogee-arched doorway has polygonal shafts with moulded capitals, and above it is a truncated window with a rounded-trefoiled head. This ensemble is flanked by strange rectangular windows with segmental extensions above and below. The upper west window, with its paired lancets, must be thirteenth century. The bell-openings are plain pointed lights, and the whole is crowned by an embattled parapet. Nave, transepts and short chancel are entirely Bateman's, ashlar-faced, and of a greenish stone, probably Downton stone. They have continuous, deep and heavy embattled parapets resting upon, of all things, a dentil cornice. Over the transepts, the central murlons are raised gable-wise. The windows consist of paired or tripled (transepts) ogee-headed lights under plain ogee hood-moulds. Each spandrel contains a 'plate tracery' quarterfoil, and in the transepts there are two set diagonally. While the parapets maintain an air of gravity, these windows display a lighthearted mien and are lovably unarchaeological.

Before stepping inside, a few words must be appended concerning the setting of Shobdon church. Bateman's house

The north side

has gone, although the stables remain, yet all is still excellently maintained. The churchyard is raised high above the lane and is planted with ornamental shrubs. The overshadowing trees create a 'dark and gloomy' prospect which would have pleased Walpole. Above on the hill stands Shobdon Arches, that eyecatcher which incorporates all that is left of the former church, two doorways and the chancel arch, their brilliant sculpture weathered beyond redemption.

The interior is an incredible fanciful display of flowing curves and half-Chinoiserie, half-Gothick detail. It is unlike anything else in England. Much of the detail is pure invention, having no medieval precedent. One might call it the Georgian equivalent of Butterfield and Teulon. The designer, while exploiting every nuance of the 'modern Gothick', must surely have been aware that he was not creating an accurate medieval interior. It is all too individualistic to be the product of ignorance alone. Within the space available, it is not possible to describe everything and a discussion of certain aspects must suffice. The strange triple responds of transept and chancel entrances look like clusters of bamboo tied together, and the equally bizarre wave-like crockets of the doorways here look as if they had been cut out of plywood. The finials, wherever they occur, are tulip-shaped and suspiciously acanthus-like. Chancel and transepts are defined by tripartite pendant ogee arches with heavy entablature-block terminations. The south transept was the Bateman family pew and has an elaborate fireplace. Even the chairs are Gothick. The windows have cusped ogee rere-arches, and between them are ogee-headed panels each with an elongated ogee quarterfoil. Indeed, it can be said that the ogee is the *lietmotif* of Shobdon. Nave and chancel roofs are coved and have rectangular panels with quarterfoil borders. There is a cornice of pendant arches. It is

The pulpit, pews, etc

A pew end

all very much like icing on a cake, and the colour scheme, white with details picked out in light blue, reinforces this impression.

As one revels in the glories of Shobdon, one's enjoyment is allayed by the memory of those great sculptures decaying up on the hill. Bateman's work has deprived future generations of the finest products created by the Herefordshire school of Norman sculpture. In its stead he gave us 'modern Gothick'. It is up to the visitor to weigh the gains and losses.

Font: c1150; plain circular bowl; circular stem with four lions *passant*.

Chairs: Of c1756, as are all the following; crocketed ogee backs with pierced arches.

Communion rail: Vertical rectangles with rounded ends connected by circles; newels with blank arches; top acanthus frieze; band of pierced quarterfoils and lozenges along base.

Communion table: Plain.

Fireplace: In south transept; an elaborate piece with a diaper background of lozenge leaves within quarterfoils; central ogee gable enclosing a quarterfoiled circle; outer shafts with heads as capitals; crocketed pinnacles.

Pews: The front of each block as communion rail; ends with arched tops and concave sides, pierced quarterfoils and pierced ogee niches below.

Pulpit (with tester): A gorgeous three-decker; the pulpit has panels with cusped lozenges and a top frieze of trefoiled arches; original velvet hangings; back-post with cusped blank arch on pilasters; tester with leaf pendants and crocketed obelisk pinnacles, a pierced cresting, crocketed ogee ribs carrying a larger pinnacle, and an elaborate ogee star underneath; reader's desk with volute-shaped supports and much cusping; clerk's desk on cusped volute brackets and ogee arches; pulpit stem with six curvy volute brackets.

Screen: To south transept; wood made to look like wrought-iron; cusped arches enclosing obelisks; cresting of inverted arches.

Screen: To north transept; as above but of wrought-iron.

West gallery: On iron columns and also two 'Tuscan' columns with leaf capitals; front with quarterfoils and a top band of elongated lozenges.

Badlesmere

A seemingly remote and quiet spot, yet the group of church, house and cottages embowered in trees is not much more than a stone's throw from a main road. The little tower-cum-bellcote waves a greeting to the visitor as he approaches across the fields from the west. It is a strange structure, in fact the whole church is a little improbable, with its flat, rendered surfaces peering through the foliage. One does not quite expect to come upon

anything so singular in this county of flint, brick and tile-hanging. The churchyard is very small but brimming with trees, laurel and other shrubs, and filled with the continuous music of birds.

The exterior is entirely rendered, and that is a finish much favoured in the early nineteenth century, though no attempt has been made to score the surface in imitation of ashlar. In many places, especially on the north side, the rendering is beginning to come apart. Despite its late Georgian appearance, the building has a history much more venerable than this. The story begins in the thirteenth century, or so it seems from the earliest extant details. They are the windows in the chancel, all lancets, single to the north and south, paired to the east. Those of the east window are extremely attenuated. The buttress here is probably coeval. It is likely that the nave is of the same time, though all features are later. Two windows were inserted in the nave about 1320; they are of two lights, and the cusped reticulated tracery confirms the date. The rest is early nineteenth century, and we begin with the tower. This is notably idiosyncratic, with its flat profile and the louvred turret perched upon the truncated pyramid roof. The turret has, in addition, a pyramid cap of its own. Windows and doorway display arch profiles of a plain chamfer and the windows are small lancets. Identical windows flank the tower. The south porch, not used as such today, is enlivened by an embattled parapet. The doorway is pointed and wooden-framed and the windows are single pointed lights. There remains only the north-west window of the nave. This has Y-tracery under a depressed arch, a typical Gothick arrangement. It is only a little more articulate than the features enumerated above. The roofs, incidentally, are of pleasantly irregular red tiles.

Upon entering, the visitor is met by an intimate and unpretentious interior that is well cared for without being repressively tidy. The walls and ceiled roof are painted white, and yellow tiles, arranged diagonally, form the floor. Most satisfying of all, perhaps, are the Georgian glazing bars in the windows, the leading creating intersections at the top. Indeed, there is nothing at Badlesmere to disturb or displease. All the fittings remain in their correct places, the reredos and communion rail, the pulpit and box pews, and there exists also a good series of text boards. Inside the theatrically-rising pews at the west end occur low benches, probably for children. The font is placed in its own pew opposite the south doorway. Of architectural features there are few, really only the broad rere-arches of the east window dying into the splays. The roof could be of the fourteenth century; it has tie-beams, octagonal crownposts with moulded capitals and four-way struts.

Bench ends: C15; two incorporated into the stalls; one has the emblem of the Trinity, the other with star and garter.
Font: C15; octagonal, plain.
Royal Arms: 1717; of George I.
Box pews: C18, as are all the following; plain panelling; brass door handles; south-east pew raised concavely; raised theatrically at west end with inset benches.
Communion rail: Slender turned balusters.
Communion table: Turned legs.
Font cover: With concave sides and a knob finial.
Pulpit: A three-decker; plain panelling; top frieze of Greek key turning into crenellation; ogee-curving stair rail.
Reredos: Very four-square; centre rising concavely and carrying a re-used medieval leaf finial; panels with Ten Commandments (basket arch), Lord's Prayer and Creed.
Stalls: With turned balusters.
Text boards: Six with eared frames.
Wall Panelling: Around the chancel; higher in sanctuary; plain; painted white. Also one hatchment.

Hatchment

Badlesmere: *Interior looking east*

Fairfield

Fairfield is a paradox indeed. For here is a church almost completely rebuilt in 1913, yet one that contains an 'unrestored' interior the like of which exists nowhere else in England. The exterior, too, appears wholly genuine, and what an exterior it is! The diminutive building, with its steep, top-heavy roofs and plump bell-turret, stands all alone on the great expanse of Romney Marsh, encircled by reed-fringed dykes. Its only companions are the flocks of sheep and the marsh frogs that leap invisibly from bank to water ahead of one's footsteps. The sheep move in slow, purposeful rhythms, the clouds trace a brisker passage across the boundless sky, and the sea winds stir reeds and tussocks into wave-like patterns that meander with the dykes. Only the church appears fixed and secure in this landscape of transient complexion, a landscape that, below its superficial outwardness, is yet secretly ancient and permanent.

The external character is governed exclusively by the seventeenth and eighteenth centuries. Windows, for example, are entirely domestic in style, wooden-framed and casemented. They snuggle under the eaves of the remarkably high roofs (especially that of the nave). The nave north window has a smaller extension to its left, the bell-turret proudly displays a beautiful covering of silver-grey shingles, set into which are horizontal grids of louvres. Red tiles cover the bold pyramid roof as they do the roofs of nave and chancel. They, in their turn, are enriched by a coating of lichens. The east gable of the nave is tile-hung, the answering chancel gable weatherboarded, and with a cusped bargeboard. The walls are of red and blue brick, not strictly arranged in a chequer pattern. Short and plain buttresses support the angles of both nave and chancel. They are called short, yet they extend right up to the eaves, indicating how low, in fact, are the walls, especially in comparison with medieval buildings. The south porch has a doorway that is completely plain.

Although the exterior is full of character, it is nothing more than a dress rehearsal for the full performance inside. It is certainly unexpected, for the internal impression is one exclusively of timber-framing. The walls are so low, and so much concealed by the furnishings, that their voice hardly makes itself heard above the chorus of woodwork. There occur

The sanctuary

tie-beams at head height on sweeping arched braces, a two-layered pseudo-tympanum between nave and chancel, unceiled rafters, and twin vestries at the west end also studded. These vestries create a little compartment for the font, beautifully lit by the west window. The only architectural features, if one can call them that, are the roofs of nave and chancel, identical, and with cambered tie-beams on wall posts, octagonal crownposts, four-way struts, and collar beams. The walls, to change the tune, are of yellow plaster left unskimmed, a pleasant textural contrast. The nave floor is of red bricks, the chancel floor of parquetry. But the *piece de resistance* is undoubtedly the ensemble of box pews, pulpit and communion rail. They are perfect in their pristine whiteness, with the edges picked out in black. The book-rest supports, and the door-handles and hinges are singularly lovely. In contrast, the dark reredos adopts a low-key, supporting role. The lighting is by candles; it could not be otherwise in this Kentish treasure-chest.

The above paragraphs have been written as if Caroe's restoration of 1913 had never happened. Yet, photographs in the church show just how much was done. Chancel, nave north wall and roof, porch and bell-turret were rebuilt entirely, and the vestries inserted internally. Caroe, however, copied exactly, and it is not difficult to disentangle what is original and what is his. It was an exceptionally sensitive job; indeed, Caroe's authenticity went as far as using medieval-type wooden pins, instead of nails, to secure the timbers. The contrast between his work and a restoration of the Tractarian decades is patently and painfully obvious. What, one shudders to think, would Butterfield have done? The change is due, of course, to William Morris; his gospel of conservation had at last begun to gain converts. Caroe rebuilt a church which was itself a post-Reformation reconstruction of a medieval timber-framed structure. Such a building existed in 1294, when a report on its poor condition was made. So perhaps the original timbering still extant can be dated to the early fourteenth century. Be that as it may, the discerning visitor will recognise beneath Caroe's gentle hand the stamp of an Arts-and-Crafts personality.

Font: c1660(?); plain heptagonal bowl; plain circular stem.
Box pews: C18; plain panelling; good door locks; an unpanelled lower pew at west end of south block, perhaps added later.
Communion rail: C18; three-sided; tall turned balusters.
Pulpit: C18; a three-decker; plain panelling; a miniature dentil frieze; book-rests on curly brackets.
Reredos: C18; a large rectangular board; two central round-arched panels with the Ten Commandments; side panels with Lord's Prayer and Creed; two Biblical quotations in painted cartouches.
Text boards: Early C19; eight oval plaques with texts; also an identical plaque inscribed 'This church ceiled and painted AD 1804'.
Communion table: c1804(?); plain square legs; pierced tracery in re-entrant angles below top.

Box pew door lock

Stelling

The lane from Upper Hardres performs a dog-leg around the church and continues southwards past a terrace of cottages, the only other buildings in the immediate vicinity. The churchyard, and its extension opposite, are well enclosed by hedges. Beyond them lie wide cornfields, stretching towards the even horizons. Interest in the churchyard is concentrated on the west side, where stand two yew trees with trunks of immense girth. Their sombre colours seem to reflect and amplify those of the church, with its dark and hard flint walls and red tiled roofs.

This, not particularly handsome, exterior has its origins in the thirteenth century, when a church of essentially the same plan (west tower, nave, south aisle, chancel) as now was erected. Presumably it replaced an earlier church. Several features remain from this initial campaign. First and foremost, we have the tower, which is structurally of this time, though altered later. Its doorway has a single-chamfered arch, ie, is extremely simple, as are the original lancet windows in the body of the church (chancel north and south, south aisle west). The south doorway, however, tries to make a show but ends up looking rather crude. It has a keeled roll on shafts carrying strangely attenuated moulded capitals. New windows were inserted during the early fourteenth century. Two (chancel east, nave north-east) have reticulated tracery, that characteristic Decorated motif. The former is lovely to look at, as is the east window of the south side, though the motifs are different here. They are cusped intersecting tracery, inset ogee sub-arches, pointed trefoils, and diagonally-set quarterfoils. These windows are the only external features which demand, and receive, lingering attention. Also early fourteenth century

are two nave north windows and the south window of the aisle; single ogee-headed lights. There is a dearth of fifteenth-century work; just the tower west window, straight-headed and with head stops. The rest is eighteenth century, viz, the tower buttresses in their present shape, the top stage of the tower, the chancel buttresses, and the south porch. The latter has a half-hipped roof and a wooden doorway trying to be Classical. The buttresses are of the angle type.

On stepping inside, the visitor first finds himself in a makeshift lobby. As one walks out of this, the pulpit and its attendant pews hit the onlooker with a bang. The ensemble is first framed by the gallery, and then by the obviously Georgian arch to the aisle. They, and the pews running towards the pulpit, create a directional confusion that takes some time to resolve. The cause of this spacial disorientation is, of course, the broad arch in place of an arcade between nave and aisle. It allows the cross axis to speak as forcefully as the east-west one. Chronologically, however, this work comes at the end of the story, and so we must turn to the thirteenth century. This manifests itself in the plain, single-chamfered tower arch, the former south arcade responds, semi-octagonal and with moulded capitals, and the thinly-chamfered chancel arch. The latter is obviously altered, and that brings us back to the eighteenth century, whose major architectural contribution is this broad segmental arch to the aisle. The bold piercing of the spandrels by plain circles effectively increases the sense of mass. The rafters of nave and aisle roofs are ceiled but the former has its worn tie-beams, crownposts and four-way struts exposed. It could be fourteenth-century. Is the chancel roof, with its thin collars on straight braces, seventeenth century?

Interior from the gallery

Communion rail

The interior is memorable for its reposeful beauty, composed of many facets. The spaciousness contributes, as does the amplitude of light, and also the high standard of cleanliness. Then there are the red tiled floors, matt, not glazed and polished as the Victorians preferred, the stone flags in the sanctuary, and the white walls and ceilings. Above all, there are the box pews, gallery and font cover so appropriately painted a pale green and white. They form the crowning achievement of the Georgian 'beautifiers'. Apropos sensitivity and appropriateness; cannot the organ be removed? Is it right that such Victorian one-upmanship should continue to blanch an otherwise perfect interior?

Font: C15 octagonal; narrow bowl with paired trefoiled arches; heavily buttressed stem.
Font cover: C17; circular; ribbed ogee dome with a leaf finial.

Box pews: C18; plain panelling; bench seats attached to fronts of south block.
Chandeliers: C18(?); single tier of branches; bulbous stem.
Communion rail: C18; sturdy, closely-set turned balusters; square newels with prism-like knobs.
Pulpit (with tester): C18; a three-decker; plain panelling; tall back-post carrying a broad, thin tester; the reader's and clerk's desks are continuous with the pews.
South gallery: C18; on Tuscan columns; front with plain pilasters and a dentil frieze below.
Stalls: C18; plain panelling; front bench with curly arm-rests.
Text boards: C18(?); lozenge-shaped; painted leaf borders. The communion table is modern.

Pilling (Old Church)

Pilling is the first of a thankfully small number of friendless churches that we are going to meet in this book. At the time of writing, slates are beginning to come off and the interior appears damp and neglected. Not yet in the deplorable condition that Skelton has to endure, it nonetheless requires determined action of some kind to ensure its survival. Like that North Riding church, Pilling stands redundant and neglected because it was replaced by a new building in the 1880s. Unlike Parracombe and Old Dilton, both of which suffered the same indignity, Pilling has not yet been taken under the wing of the Redundant Churches Fund. The post-1880 story, however, is more fantastical than this. The village was given a new church on condition that the old one would be demolished. The latter was not so treated, but it was erased from the Church Commissioners' 'account book' and thus, officially, Pilling old church does not exist! Therefore it cannot be declared redundant. It is high time that such bureaucratic nonsense was resolved and the future of this particular fragment of our architectural heritage secured.

Paradoxically, the churchyard is still used for burials. It is quite a large churchyard, open, but with a splendid avenue of junipers leading to the door of the church. Amongst the headstones the nineteenth century predominates, which allows for an effective contrast with the unspoilt character of the church. The grass is not cut short, yet contains surprisingly few wild flowers.

The church consists of a nave and chancel in one with a bold bellcote above the west gable. This west wall, and the north side also, are rendered, but the rest is of exposed stone, a rich brown stone against which occur great patches of lichen. There exists a brick-like quality in the size of the stones, especially noticeable in the way they have been cut and laid in a header-and-stretcher fashion. The angles have alternating quoins. The slate roof is badly in need of repair. The bellcote has two segmentally-arched openings with plain capitals and a broken segmental pediment carrying a ball finial. It is entirely pre-Georgian, or perhaps one should say pre-Palladian, in character. While there is nothing out-of-the-ordinary about this feature, the south doorway offers a strange and very rustic solution to the problem of composing with Classical vocabulary. The broad frame is essentially continuous but is broken by applied 'Ionic' capitals of a most primitive kind. The keystone carries the date 1717. Clearly, a true understanding of the orders had not yet penetrated this remote corner of Lancashire. Above is a sundial dated 1766. Above, yet again, is a window that is not a lunette but, if one ignores the block-like capitals, takes the form of a stilted arch. The main windows are tall and round-arched and contain a mullion running up against the apex. The chancel east window is distinguished by being given two mullions. On the north side two tiers occur, the lower rectangular, the upper lunette-shaped. This arrangement may date from 1812-3, when a new gallery was installed, a supposition supported by Gothick elements in the glazing bars.

Exploration of the interior is tinged with the sadness of visible neglect. Urgent repairs are needed, especially at the

Exterior from the south

Interior looking east

west end, where there is a gaping hole above the gallery. Down below, one senses that the church is being used as a convenient store for graveyard equipment. It is all extremely regrettable, for here is an interior full of quiet character, with flat plastered ceiling, white walls, and a lovely view through the east window to a screen of foliage. The furnishings, too, are pleasantly varied, and that archetypal feature of many an unrestored church, the cast-iron stove with its flue soaring through the roof, stamps the whole with an approving seal. The floors are of stone and the woodwork displays several gradations of colour; lighter in the gallery, darker in the pews, and the pulpit adopting a middle stance. A makeshift baptistry encloses the font, employing pannelling re-used from elsewhere, and set diagonally across, instead of forming a square, which is the usual thing. The high and stately galleries, although dominant, do not overcrowd.

Surely this perfect example of the 'prayer-book' *genre* is worth saving for future generations?

Baptistry panelling: C17(?); plain, with knobs; re-used from a pew?

Benches: C17(?); the ends with plain curly tops; open backs; numbered; very rustic.

Box pews: One dated 1719; plain panelling.

Commandment boards: c1719; frames with the usual raised lunette tops.

Communion rail: c1719; three-sided; rounded corners; elegant turned balusters.

Communion table: c1719; heavy turned legs.

Font: c1719; of stone; tulip-shaped bowl; moulded stem; moulded base with leaf at the corners.

Pulpit: c1719; a three-decker; plain panelling.

Royal Arms: 1719; of George I.

West & north galleries: 1812-3; wooden Tuscan columns; plain panelled fronts; stairs with square balusters and a gate across.

Box pews: c1812-3; in the north-west corner; plain panelling; lighter wood as galleries.

Communion rail: detail

King's Norton

Interior looking east

As one approaches King's Norton, the church appears as the predominant building of the village, raised upon an eminence and visible from afar. From a few fields away it looks plausibly medieval; the tower certainly convinces, yet there is something about that rectangular block of a nave which does not ring true. Also, there is no visible chancel. As the building looms larger, the mystery resolves itself, for here is a church not of the Middle Ages but of the mid eighteenth century. A church, moreover, that ranks as one of the most important of the early Gothic Revival — still Gothick, of course, but of a seriousness of purpose far in advance of Shobdon and the like. Gone are the thin ogee mouldings, the quarterfoils, the playful Rococo forms. Instead, there are now proper string-courses, a correct system of buttressing, and tracery motifs copied accurately from neighbouring churches. Yet Shobdon had only been finished a year when King's Norton was started.

The church was built for William Fortrey, Esquire, by John Wing the Younger (1728-94). It was begun in 1757 and completed in 1761. Wing's father, also called John, had built Galby in 1741 for the same patron, less accurate but pointing the way towards his son's own attempt. The Wings were a local family of mason-builders gifted with a flair for accurate observation. The tower has angle buttresses and is divided into four stages by archaeologically-correct string courses whose motifs are quarterfoils, mouchette wheels and cusped triangles. These string-courses are carried across the buttresses. The ground stage contains a large quarterfoiled circle, so different in effect from the universal bare quarterfoils of Gothick buildings. Above is a two-light window with reticulated tracery, and above that a cusped lozenge. The bell-openings consist of paired two-lighters, with transom, reticulated tracery and ogee hood-moulds. Only the latter appear a little too thin for comfort. A corbel table supports the parapet which has tall panelled and crocketed pinnacles and pierced quarterfoils. The way in which each stage is differentiated, with the emphasis of height placed upon the uppermost, is correctly medieval.

The nave displays seven bays of identical fenestration, each being separated by buttresses carrying pinnacles identical to those of the tower. The windows, too, are like the bell-openings, tall, of two lights, with the same tracery and hood-moulds. Above, a frieze of cusped triangles and a parapet of pierced quarterfoils run all along. They are stopped at the east end by taller pinnacles. These link up with the east facade and its great window of a cathedral magnificence. It is a *tour-de-force* in the exploitation of geometrical tracery, not the ordered classic tracery of, say, Westminster Abbey, but the freer varieties of about 1290. Here we find unencircled rounded and pointed trefoils, with a large group enclosed within a circle as the climax of the composition. The lights are grouped two-five-two to create a broad design of really three separate windows, and beneath these effulgent geometric reflections one can sense the ghost of a Venetian window. Nonetheless, to reproduce so perfectly such complex forms was a major achievement in 1757. Wing's source may have been Goadby Marwood, where similar motifs occur, but both the centre and its side parts are almost identical to windows in the chapter house vestibule of York Cathedral.

One enters the church under the tower, whose doorway is approached up a flight of steps with a balustrade, the only Classical feature of the exterior. The interior comes as a profound shock. It is overwhelmingly moving in its Puritan starkness, the exact antithesis of the exterior. Elaboration is eschewed everywhere; bare are the pews, bare the pulpit, bare the walls and flooring, and bare even the reredos. Even the usual texts are absent. The architecture, too, is pared down to a minimum. In short, there exists nothing which might attract attention away from prayer and sermon. It would have pleased Cromwell immensely but could only bring a disapproving outcry from Laud. The one concession to display is the black-and-white marble paving of the sanctuary. So the colour scheme is one of brown furnishings, cream walls and sandy stone flooring. The furnishings are of Norwegian oak, and their arrangement at the east end is unique. The pulpit is placed centrally, right in front of the altar (how Pugin would have hated this!) the only undisturbed example in England of this characteristically Puritan plan. Another exists at St John, Chichester, but there the setting has been changed. A pair of Gothick gates flank the pulpit and lead into a 'chancel' with family pews placed longitudinally, as in a college chapel. These gates, and the communion rail also, are the only furnishings with medieval detail. The rest are restrainedly Classical. The roof has tie-beams on braces with pierced trefoils in the spandrels; the brackets may belong to repairs carried out after the spire had collapsed in 1850. Before this disaster, the rafters had been ceiled.

To sum up, the great interest of King's Norton lies in the emotional and visual contrast between exterior and interior, and in the arrangement of the furnishings. Despite Wing's scholarly gothicisms, one remembers the church as the *locus classicus* amongst Georgian preaching houses.

The furnishings are all of 1757-61.
Baptismal pew: Under the gallery; just bench seats around the font.
Box pews: Plain panelling.
Chancel gates: Flanking the pulpit; two tiers of pierced panel tracery separated by a band of reticulation.
Communion rail: As gates but with a leaf frieze.
Communion table: Square fluted legs; top frieze of Greek key.
Family pews: Arranged college-wise; two tiers each side; plain panelling; backs with panelled pilasters and dentils.
Pulpit: A three-decker; square pulpit with plain panelling, detached fluted Tuscan columns at angles, and a dentil frieze; carved stairs with fluted balusters; reader's and clerk's desks with plain panelling, the front corners bowed.
Reredos: Central pediment on panelled pilasters; panels with egg-and-dart frames; dentil frieze.
Royal Arms: Of George III.
West gallery: On fluted Tuscan columns; also fluted pilasters, front with triglyphs, short pilasters and dentils.
The font is C19; the original was destroyed when the spire fell.

The pulpit

Staunton Harold

'In the year 1653 when all things Sacred were throughout ye nation Either demolisht or profaned Sir Robert Shirley, Barronet, Founded this church; Whose singular praise it is, to have done the best thing in ye worst times, and hoped them in the most callamitous. The righteous shall be had in everlasting remembrance.' Thus the inscription above the west doorway, for Staunton Harold is the memorial to a young man's gallant stand against the Puritan regime of Cromwell. When Cromwell heard of the church, he charged Sir Robert to raise a regiment on the strength that, if he could afford to erect so splendid a building, it would not be beyond his resources to find funds for the Protector's army. Sir Robert refused and was imprisoned in the Tower for his pains, where he died in 1665 at the age of twenty-seven. His church was not completed until 1665.

Sir Robert Shirley was an ardent Royalist and a staunch supporter of the Anglican Church in the Laudian sense. A recent ancestor had been a recusant Catholic, but the family had reverted to the Church of England before Sir Robert inherited. In building Staunton Harold he was, perhaps, paying tribute to Laud and Charles I, but above all he was making a defiant gesture against the joyless regime he hated so much, a regime completely antipathetic towards Laud's desire for 'beauty in holiness'. No other pre-Victorian church in England reflects so felitiously one man's beliefs and philosophy, nor rivals it as the consummation of Laud's ideals. Architecturally, too, it is outstanding as one of only a handful of churches built during the Commonwealth (Holy Trinity, Berwick-upon-Tweed is another) and certainly the finest. It is also extremely important stylistically, for reasons we will come to in a moment.

The setting is exquisite; church and house stand together upon a lawn overlooking a reed-fringed lake. The church is so self-assured that it makes the house appear less imposing. It has its churchyard defined by a substantial stone wall, buttressed at the corners, and is accompanied by a ragged Scots pine to its left, a more compact tree to the right. Here man and Nature seem in perfect equilibrium. The layman will be forgiven for accepting Staunton Harold as a genuine late medieval church. The forms are correct, or appear correct, and the whole is as noble as any church in Somerset or the Cotswolds. The building consists of an ample west tower, a broad nave with clerestory, north and south aisles, and chancel. It is embattled throughout, and the parapet of the clerestory has pierced quarterfoils in lozenge panels. The buttresses carry prominent crocketed pinnacles. The east and west windows of both aisles have cusped Y-tracery, the side windows here, and all chancel windows, cusped intersecting tracery. Those of the clerestory, to change the tune, are straight-headed and have cusped panel tracery. The three-stage tower has angle buttresses, a west window that is convincingly Perpendicular, paired two-light bell-openings with more Y-tracery, and an embattled parapet with crocketed pinnacles and intermediate fleurs-de-lis. All this is Gothic, but the west doorway's surround betrays the real date. Here we find paired termini pilasters linked by swags held in the mouths of lion masks, an entablature, a pair of Mannerist standing angels, and the inscription in a framework of volutes, ribbons, and a rich coat of arms.

The Gothic elements cannot be dismissed simply in terms of Survival; they are employed far too consciously for that. So here a few words concerning the whole question of Gothic Survival versus Revival need to be interpolated. Generally, a feature can be considered Survival if it is the unconscious continuation of the late Perpendicular interpreted in an ever more simplified or 'debased' manner. If, conversely, that feature displays motifs from the earlier Middle Ages, or Perpendicular ones used with a full understanding of their original character, then it becomes a case of Revival. At Staunton Harold we find Y and intersecting tracery, ie, motifs of about 1300, combined with other windows, etc, and a set of proportions, that belong to the fifteenth and early sixteenth century. All are used deliberately to create a symbol, the symbol of the English Church reformed, not the Protestant Church founded in the Reformation. The historical background clinches the matter; the church is pre-eminently a Gothic Revival building and must be judged in the context of certain work in Oxford, St Katherine Cree in London, and other buildings mainly of the 1630s. Amongst them all, Staunton Harold stands supreme.

The impression of the interior is one of High Church richness. Here occur a full range of arcades, a spacious and quite deep chancel screened off from the nave, and an altar correctly raised. Admittedly, the usual box pews appear, and they are beautifully made, but the pulpit does not dominate, being self-effacingly placed to one side of the chancel arch. Indeed, the eye is drawn to Bakewell's superb screen and up to the unexpected boarded roofs with their allegorical paintings. These are incredibly naive, but loveable just for that reason. All more-or-less identical, their theme may be Creation out of Chaos. The clouds end up looking as if they were strings of balloons and other festive decorations. The artists were Zachery and Samuel Kyrk for the nave, a Mr Lovett for the rest. The chancel is distinguished by a floor of grey marble laid lozenge-wise. The nave's stone floor is nicely irregular. The three-bay arcades have double-chamfered arches, octagonal piers, and moulded capitals. The piers are panelled in wood; indeed, the whole interior is lined with panelling, a fine unifying effect. Chancel and tower arches are as the arcades; that of the tower is also panelled. The furnishings were made by William Smith; their style is Carolean, not Gothic.

The recent history of the estate is this. During World War II the house was occupied by the army. Afterwards, proposals for open-cast mining were formulated. Then, at the eleventh hour, the Cheshire Homes stepped in, acquired the house and park, and the church was given to the National Trust. It is fitting that this loveliest of churches should be in the latter's discriminating and thoughtful care.

Altar frontal: c1660-5, as are all the following; a gold motif of IHS in a sun. Also original cushions.
Box pews: Plain panelling, the upper tier flanked by demi-balusters; S-shaped brass candlesticks.
Chancel panelling: Paired blank arches with diamond rustication and pendants between tapering pilasters with strapwork and cherubs' heads; cornice with leaf volutes, egg-and-dart, leaf trailing, shields and rosettes.
Communion table: A turned leg placed centrally at either end supported by volutes; base bar in the form of a horizontally-placed oval.
Font: Of stone; a large, plain, circular bowl on a circular stem.
Font cover: Circular base; square cover with knobs at the corners on miniature detached balusters; convex top with four volute ribs carrying a knob finial.
Nave panelling: Plain; top with lozenges.
Pulpit: A two-decker; blank arches set in frames with open curly pediments; also lozenges and diamond rustication; book-rest on modillions; reader's desk with blank arches

Interior looking west

Nave ceiling: detail

framed by fluted pilaster.

Tower Screen: Large pierced central archway with diamond rustication; side lights ditto; top with pierced leaf scrolls; panelled base with ovals.

West gallery: Panelled pilasters with attached balusters; also ovals, etc. Above is the Shirley arms in an open and broken segmental pediment.

Organ case: 1686; tripartite projections.

Chancel screen: 1711; by Robert Bakewell; wrought-iron; mainly vertical motifs with much scroll and leaf; cresting with Royal Arms. Also four hatchments.

Hannah-cum-Hagnaby

The hamlet of Hannah consists of nothing more than the church, a farm, and one or two cottages. They form an island in a sea of cornfields, those interminable Lincolnshire cornfields that extend to every horizon. The land rises and falls again just sufficiently to produce a slight eminence where the church stands. In the churchyard, headstones fight for supremacy with the long grass, and bow to each other, or lean apart. Tall trees form an enclosing ring, completely dominating the church, which adopts a low profile under the foliage. The fortuitous juxtaposition of the pantiles, with their regular undulations looking like waves on a choppy sea, and the leaves above, is especially gratifying.

The exterior is unpretentious in a chapel-like way, the contours and details utilitarian. Only the tilers enjoyed a field day, though even they were employing a time-honoured, unconsciously sensitive method. The walls are of greenstone, and they comprise a building of a nave and chancel in one, with a timber bell-turret set back a little from the gable, together with a lower west porch entered from the south. Plan and

elevation remind one of Leweston, although that church, of course, is much more urbane than Hannah. The bell-turret is a delicate piece, the sides open with a little cusping, the pyramid cap and base weatherboarded. The side windows are round-arched and have plain, somewhat heavy frames with abaci blocks and keystones. Their character is early Georgian, not that of the date of the church, which is 1753. The east window is Venetian and has broad divisions between each light. The proportions of the west porch are identical to those of the nave, though on a much smaller scale. Above in the west gable is a blank lunette. The porch entrance has a pointed arch which looks like a later insertion, rather than something older re-used. Inside the porch occurs the only medieval feature, ie, the doorway into the church, fifteenth century with continuous mouldings. Here also can be seen two sections of former responds with figures one above the other.

The interior is humble, unaffected and friendly, happily crowded by the substantial box pews and communion rail. There is hardly room for anything else; even the onlooker will feel that he does not belong in this domain of timber. Yet this very overcrowding creates a stronger feeling of intimacy than could be experienced in a more spacious church. The brick floors are of a yellow hue, the walls and flat plastered ceiling white. One feature above all others tells of the Georgian century's attitudes towards the requisites of worship. The visitor will look in vain for the conventional free-standing font. Instead, he will find a simple basin boxed into the corner of a

Exterior from the south

The communion rail

pew and provided with its own little cover. Let nothing interfere with the essentials of a preaching house and an auditorium for the delivery of the sermon.

A short while ago, the long-term future of Hannah was in doubt, but now the church is maintained in an excellent state of preservation. Fresh flowers and clean carpets provide witness to a former rector's gallant fight against abandonment. Though past retirement, he doggedly opposed the then anti-preservationist Bishop of Lincoln's desire to reduce the number of churches. The rector won, and vowed his church would never be locked.

Box pews: Of c1753, as are the following; plain panelling.
Commandment boards: Raised lunette tops.
Communion rail: Three-sided, with an extension on the left; the centre projects convexly; closely-set turned balusters.
Font: A basin boxed into the corner of a pew.
Font cover: Circular, like a dish cover; knob finial.
Pulpit (with tester): A two-decker; plain panelling; back-post with volutes; tester with bands of leaf; stairs with turned balusters; large section for both reader and clerk.
The two chandeliers are probably C19. The communion table is recent.

Hannah-cum-Hagnaby: *Font cover*

Langton-by-Partney

The churchyard is a rough hump of grassland, kept in trim by sheep. It levels out towards the south-east where broad views appear. On the north side a steep bank drops to the lane and a stream, and from there the church appears unexpectedly bold upon the crest. The view through the trees to the clean, orderly walls of the church is exquisite. Of brick also is the former rectory on the opposite side of the lane. For contrast, a little to the east stands a sweet cottage orné with a thatched roof.

Langton is a curious church; a plain rectangle capped by a deeply-projecting roof carrying the most improbable of bell-turrets. The whole possesses the quality of a toy constructed from childrens' building blocks. The roof especially looks as if it had been glued into place. Its overhanging pedimental gable reminds one of Inigo Jones's St Paul, Covent Garden. Indeed, the general contours of the church are, no doubt, a distant reflection of that momentous design. The external features hardly exploit the third dimension, so little disturbs the basic planes of the walls. Each side has five bays of plain round-arched windows with keystones and a fine set of glazing bars. Above, a lightly-indicated string-course runs along, and above that occur shallow, sunk rectangular panels. So this upper area is meant to represent a parapet. The corners have alternating quoins of stone. The east wall has three blank windows and,

above them, three segmental-arched niches. On the entrance front a variation on this theme occurs, whereby the central blank window is replaced by a doorway with a triangular pediment, and the middle niche under the gable by a keyed-in horizontally-set oval. All this cannot be precisely dated, although it is likely to be of about 1725. But the bell-turret is younger by exactly a century, having been erected in 1825 as a replacement of the original lead-covered one. It is octagonal, remarkably blunt at the top, and each face displays two circular openings stamped into the brickwork. These occuli possess a Vanbrughian quality: was this great architect's influence still felt in the north at so recent a date?

A spacial surprise awaits the visitor as he opens the door. The exterior's regular fenestration seems to imply an unsubdivided room, but behind the west front is a small vestibule, like the space under a tower. It delays revealing the delights of the interior just enough to garnish anticipation with an intensified excitement. Twin stairs lead up to the gallery, and it is worth ascending, not only to view the nave from up there, but to climb higher into the ringing chamber to see the abstract shapes of the clock mechanism. It is, in any case, fun to explore the various levels and compartments of this unexpected 'westwork'. The inner doorway, with its panelled surround, opens to disclose one of the most perfect 'prayer-book' interiors anywhere, perfect, that is, except for the oversized organ in the north-east corner.

What attracts specially is the seating arranged as in a college chapel. Few churches preserve this plan, which may once have been quite common. There are three rising tiers on each side, those on the south interrupted by the superb three-decker pulpit. At the east end, these pews come forward in a concave

Interior looking east

The clock mechanism

curve, thus foreshortening perspective and emphasizing the sanctuary. The reredos spreads itself from wall to wall and is sunk concavely behind the altar. This niche (it is too shallow to be called an apse) is again unannounced outside. Its effect is heightened above cornice level by the two volutes which project at right-angles, and by the panelling of the ceiling. This includes a roundel with the Dove. In any case, the niche walls protrude slightly in front of the side parts. The ceiling is imperceptibly coved, and has a central rectangle with a border of Greek key and a cornice with dentils and egg-and-dart. It is painted white whereas the walls are a pale lime green. Do not overlook the gradation in the flooring as it progresses from west to east. In the nave the stone flags are laid in a rectangular formation, in the chancel lozenge-wise, and the development concludes with a black-and-white marble pavement in the sanctuary.

Font: Later C14; octagonal; bowl with window tracery designs; stem with tracery-headed panels.

Box pews: Of c1725, as are all the following; arranged college-wise; fronts with plain panelling between fluted pilasters; some seats have curly ends.

Communion rail: Three-sided; turned balusters.

Font cover: Octagonal base; ribbed ogee dome with a ball finial.

Pulpit (with tester): A three-decker; tall, narrow panels between fluted angle pilasters; triglyph frieze; slim panelled back-post; deep tester with triglyphs with a star in inlay work; staircase with turned balusters; reader's and clerk's desks with plain panelling.

Reredos: Returned a short distance along north and south walls; concave centre with fluted Corinthian pilasters; plain panelling; dentil cornice; a small segmental pediment with three pierced, spiky finials.

West gallery: On two sturdy fluted Tuscan columns; plainly panelled front. Also three hatchments.

Well

Well enjoys a picturesqueness of setting unmatched by any other church in this book. Instead of standing among cottages or alongside a country house, this small, temple-like church becomes the prime focus of a park landscape of contrived naturalness. It stands upon the brow of a hill and overlooks a lake, or rather a chain of lakes, and the considerably larger house. The latter was erected about 1725, the church in 1733,

The pulpit

and if the former date is correct this placing of a church as an eye-catcher or picturesque object in the landscape is singularly early. Gunton in Norfolk, by Robert Adam, is a much later example (1769) that comes to mind. To reach the church one follows the drive as it crosses the lakes by a short length of causeway and then winds upwards through the Borrominesque gatepiers (probably by Archer), finally coming to rest among the trees on the ridge. The view from up there is splendid, with the lakes dispersed on the left, and the house to their right aligned on the portico of the church.

In its external character Well resembles Langton-by-Partney. Here occurs the same combination of a rectangular body covered by an overhanging, barn-like roof. But Well is only two bays long and is the proud possessor of a full-blown portico instead of a utilitarian projecting gable end. The portico has a broad pediment on four Tuscan columns and, against the back wall, Tuscan pilasters, a pair of niches in rectangular frames, and a doorway with a detached entablature. It is a direct translation of Inigo Jones's St Paul, Covent Garden (1631-8), which is itself derived from Scamozzi's illustration of the 'Etruscan barn'. The cupola above is Victorian but indistinguishable from many of the previous century. Though perfectly acceptable in itself, it perpetuates the painful ambiguity of a vertical feature standing upon a pediment introduced by James Gibbs at St Martin-in-the-Fields. It is surprising how popular and influential Gibbs' illogical arrangement proved to be, even winning followers in America. The cupola has six stone Tuscan columns carrying a wooden entablature and an ogee dome with a finial. The side windows are round-arched and have white keystones and abaci, and wooden Y-tracery which must be a later insertion. The east window is Venetian, again with Y-tracery.

Unlike Langton, the door at Well opens immediately into the nave, and into one of the most deeply satisfying unrestored interiors of all. It lies one step ahead of Langton in the sense that it is not disturbed by the all-too-frequent introduction of a nineteenth-century organ. The clarity of furnishings and architecture speak for themselves. Egg-and-dart borders frame the side windows. The east window has panelled reveals, egg-and-dart friezes, vertical panels with leaf borders between the lights, garlands above the side lights, and a cherub's head keystone. The ceiling has as its centrepiece a circle, open at the cardinal points and enclosing a quarterfoil of tulips which, in turn, contains a roundel with acanthus leaf and grapes. The circle is surrounded by ribbons and has cherubs' heads in the spandrels. There is also an acanthus boss in a roundel above the altar. The cornice is refined and very beautiful. From bottom to top its motifs are: two leaf bands, garlands, egg-and-dart, enriched modillions. The ceiling is white, the walls pale green, ie, just as at Langton. Rush matting, very appropriately, covers the diagonally-set stone flags.

On several occasions comparisons have been drawn between Well and Langton-by-Partney; one more still remains. The pews and pulpit are practically identical, not only in being arranged college-wise, but also in their motifs. The same pilasters occur here, the same curly ends to the seats. Only in two minor ways can a change be detected; they are the introduction of a dentil frieze in the tester and slight differences in the staircase balusters. Both sets must come from a single joiner's shop. It is inevitable that the two churches will be compared, so similar are they in many respects. So the particularising of each building's individual strengths and weaknesses will now be attempted. Well's setting cannot even begin to be matched by Langton's, though

Box pew: detail

the latter's exterior is more likable because it is less formal and correct. Well lacks the internal subdivisions which add interest at Langton, but is superior in other ways mentioned above. The sanctuary arrangement at Langton, however, is superior; the pulpit at Well, though a twin of Langton, seems just that little more stately and memorable. Now let the reader decide.

Box pews: Of c1733, as are all the following; arranged college-wise; plain panelling between fluted pilasters; curly ends to the seats.
Chancel panelling: Narrow vertical panelling, the centre eight panels flanked by fluted pilasters.
Commandment boards: Round-arched; leafy borders.
Communion rail: Slim turned balusters.
Family pews: A pair flanking the altar; as box pews.
Pulpit (with tester): A three-decker; pulpit with vertical panels between fluted angle pilasters; triglyph frieze; tall narrow, plainly panelled back-post; tester with triglyphs and dentils; stairs with turned balusters; reader's and clerk's desks with plain panelling.
Reredos: Small but rich; central feature with imitation concave doors set inside a blank arch on fluted pilasters, the doors with leaf in square panels, a fan above; this is contained within a recess flanked by fluted Tuscan pilasters, carrying an entablature with triglyphs; lower curving-down side pieces with similar pilasters.
Royal Arms: Of George II.
West gallery: Plain panelling; the centre projects slightly. The font, a wooden baluster, has recently been stolen.

Little Stanmore

Little Stanmore is the *locus classicus,* in ecclesiastical terms, of the continental Baroque translated onto English soil. For comparisons, one must turn to Wren's Painted Hall at Greenwich Hospital, rather than Great Whitley in Worcestershire or the major English Baroque churches. Here was attempted a synthesis of painting, architecture and concealed lighting in imitation of the great Baroque artists of Italy, Germany, etc. That the attempt failed no one will deny; the reasons will be discussed in a moment.

The church was rebuilt by James Brydges, Earl of Carnarvon, in 1715. He was the son of the 8th Lord Chandos of Sudeley but had become amazingly rich in his own right through being Marlborough's Paymaster-General. He received his earldom in 1714. The Canons estate came to him through his first wife and on it he erected a princely mansion. He was made Duke of Chandos in 1719. Talman, John James, Gibbs and John Price were all employed on the house at various times. The paintings were executed by Bellucci, the plasterwork by Bagutti; even Handel became his *Kapellmeister* for two years, hence the Chandos Anthem. After Chandos died the house was demolished and much of its contents sold. Only the church remained as a somewhat tired witness to his short-lived regime of grandeur and ostentation.

None of this will be apparent to the visitor as he makes his way along Whitchurch Lane with its accompaniment of any-town suburbia. The church, seemingly no different from many another country church partly rebuilt during the eighteenth century, stands broadside to the road in a churchyard crowded with tombs. There is, in addition, an ample supply of greenery, a natural oasis in an urban world. The west tower survives from the medieval building. It has diagonal buttresses, an embattled parapet of brick (the rest is flint and stone), and bell-openings with that broadish Y-tracery which occurs occasionally in buildings of the early sixteenth century. There is also a prominent polygonal stair-turret rising higher and given its own battlements.

The rest is all Chandos, including the west front of the tower with its circular window above a doorway whose segmental arch rests upon volutes. The church has a plain parapet above an equally reticent cornice. All details are picked out in stone and contrast effectively with the brickwork. There are three bays of windows between two projecting frontispieces, one for the entrance, the other a shallow transept. The windows have surrounds of the utmost severity, just plain, unmoulded bands, sills and aprons. The entrance facade is the showpiece of the exterior. It has a doorway with a moulded segmental arch linked to a detached hood by a tall keystone. The hood acts as the sill of a window which takes the form of a stilted arch, or, in other words, a normal window cut short. This *ensemble* is flanked by tall angle pilasters whose order (Tuscan in reality) is hardly indicated. The transeptal projection has the same pilasters. The 'chancel' has a window as before, and an east facade with two niches, a pediment enclosing a circular window, and angle pilasters. On the north side the Chandos mausoleum interferes. It contains Carpentier's monument to the Duke but, wisely perhaps, remains firmly locked. The mausoleum is of a redder brick. All the details are of a severity reminiscent of Hawksmoor, although he had nothing to do with Chandos and Canons. John James has been suggested as the designer of the church; his is the most likely name.

Since entry is from the south, initial impact belongs to the the paintings on the nave north wall. Attention, however, will soon be drawn eastwards, for what appeared to be a normal chancel outside reveals itself as a retrochoir-in-miniature beyond the altar. It is lit dramatically from the side, thus illuminating the paintings and throwing the organ into high relief. The altar stands below a proscenium arch, and the whole is indeed theatrical, emotional and fully Baroque. Yet, how tame it is in comparison even with Greenwich, let alone Weltenburg or the Transparente in Toledo Cathedral. But, then, how could a style so inextricably linked with the Counter-Reformation and Catholic *bravura* succeed in moderate, reticent, Anglican England? It is the same with the paintings. Despite the illusionism, window openings remain firmly separated from walls, walls from ceiling. There is nothing of that symphonic integration of architecture, sculpture and painting which is the great achievement of the Asams, Neumann, and the rest.

The proscenium arch or screen has a flat segmental coffered arch with drapes. It rests upon sections of entablature supported by beautiful wooden Corinthian columns, paired in depth, and also square attached columns. The entablature displays enriched modillions, egg-and-dart, and dentils, and above the flanking paintings appear wreaths and cherubs' heads. The nave is covered by a segmental barrel vault with penetrations over the transepts. Its scheme of decoration is organised into transverse bands separated by strips of coffering. Along the ridge run enriched roundels, along the side scenes in surrounds with the familiar raised lunette tops. The spaces between these parallel groups are filled with leaf, etc. After all this licence the furnishings appear modest to the point of rectitude. It is strange that they are not treated as lavishly as the decoration. Little Stanmore remains unique as far as England is concerned, but the layman must be wary of granting it an omnipotence which it does not possess or, indeed, deserve.

All furnishings are of c1715.

Box pews: Plain panelling; numbered.

Ceiling Paintings: The Miracles of Christ along sides; the Adoration of Jehovah above the altar; all by Louis Laguerre.

Chancel gates: Wrought-iron; spikes; three vertical motifs with scrolls.

Communion rail: Wrought-iron; three-sided, the sides and front connected by sunk convex sections; symmetrical vertical motifs with scrolls.

Font: A marble baluster; octagonal gadrooned bowl; the base also gadrooned.

Nave wall paintings: St John and St Peter against transeptal responds: St Mark and St Matthew between Faith, Hope and Charity on north side, St John and St Luke on south side; the allegories stand against feigned niches enclosed by pilasters carrying broken segmental pediments; the saints stand against flat backgrounds enclosed by architectural frames with segmental tops; saints on south side as allegories; cartouches, etc, below figures; monochrome; all by Laguerre.

Organ: Semi-circular projections with leaf and pairs of cherubs' heads; pierced leaf friezes; by Gerard Smith.

Proscenium paintings: The Nativity; the Descent from the Cross; by Antonio Bellucci.

Pulpit: A three-decker; plain panelling; stairs with twisted balusters; reader's and clerk's desks with wrought-iron fronts.

Retrochoir paintings: The Giving of the Law; the Sermon on the Mount; by Laguerre.

Stalls: Wrought-iron fronts as communion rail; top with heavy fretwork.

West gallery: The Chandos family pew; tripartite, with a broad central arch and lower, narrower side arches; plain

The east end

Little Stanmore: *Wall painting: Hope*

panelled pilasters; apsed interior with semi-domes; the
lower screen repeats the arrangement above; painting of
the Transfiguration by Bellucci.
The altar is recent and too overtly neo-Renaissance.

Warham St Mary

Interior looking west

The church stands in a beautiful churchyard surrounded by trees, as if it were a clearing in a wood. It is an informal churchyard, the gravestones rising directly from the turf, with few graves visible. The main visual contrast lies in the hard flint walls of the church, with their various blues and greys, seen against the multitudinous greens of the foliage.

The external aspect of the church is a typical East Anglian one; the thin and utilitarian-looking forms and details, the diagonal buttresses of the tower rising in many set-offs, the occasional use of flushwork, all help to differentiate the building from those of the stone belt. Although the church, like so many in this region, looks Perpendicular now, it has its origins in the first half of the twelfth century. Of that Norman era only the blocked north doorway remains. It has one order of shafts carrying single-scalloped capitals and a roll moulding in the arch. A general rebuilding took place during the thirteenth century. Nave and chancel were enlarged and a deep south porch added. The porch is faced with knapped flints, that characteristic East Anglian motif, and the doorway has one order of slim shafts carrying moulded capitals and also continuous mouldings. The doorway inside has hollows dying into the responds. Round the corner in the nave west wall occurs a single lancet window crammed into the space between the tower and the south-west angle. It is an odd position and seems to presuppose a tower earlier than the present one, unless the lancet is re-set from elsewhere. But it is far too small to have been the west window of a towerless church. The most striking external feature, rare but not unique, is the priest's doorway. This is set into a little gabled porch from the apex of which rises a buttress. The effect is that of a large open fireplace and chimney-breast. Shafting and mouldings are as the porch doorway. Alongside is a window with Y-tracery. Its character is Early English rather than Decorated, and so all this thirteenth-century work can perhaps be dated to about 1260-80.

The early fourteenth century contributed the tower, though it may be a rebuilding of an earlier one (see above). Separate stages divided by string-courses are absent. The rather crude two-light bell-openings each contain a basic reticulation unit. The embattled parapet displays a rough flushwork pattern of diamond shapes and may well be, though not necessarily, fifteenth century. This century, the great age of the Perpendicular style, brought a number of changes in the fenestration. The tower was given a new, enlarged west window, as were the north and south walls of the nave and the east wall of the chancel. They are all of three lights, with panel tracery, and differ only in minor ways. The tracery of the tower window is more elegantly formed and displays more cusping than that of the others. It could be late fourteenth century rather than fifteenth century. There is, in addition, one further window of this period in the chancel south wall. It is again of three cusped lights (not ogee) but differs in being straight-headed. This latter feature does not necessarily indicate a later date. Below runs a plinth with flint-and-stone chequer and, as this begins only east of the priest's doorway, suggests that the fifteenth-century work included an extension of the chancel. The sole contribution of the eighteenth century is the brick north chapel, built by the Turner family some time before 1780. Its windows contain typical Gothick Y-tracery.

The interior impresses us with its clarity and airiness. It is, with its untrammelled spaces, its bare whitewashed walls, its stone floors, and unaffected charm, almost an archetypal East Anglian interior. Only the screens and hammerbeam roofs are absent. Instead, we have that universal Georgian contribution, the plastered ceiling, and one unusual addition, the foreign stained glass imported by the then rector, the Rev. W.H. Langton. The glass introduces just enough colour to animate the entire building. Langton became rector in 1790 and it was he who 'beautified' the church in 1800-1. He ceiled the roofs, giving them simple barrel vaults, re-plastered the walls, and

The font

replaced whatever furnishings there may have been with a suite of box pews and a truly splendid three-decker pulpit. He kept the chancel clear, except for the introduction of wall panelling, and after the all-too-frequent paraphernalia of most churches how thankful we are for his restraint. The ceilings have roundels with a fan and leaf enrichment, three for the nave, one for the chancel. The slightly earlier north chapel is a strange, unadorned room, set apart from the church and with a sad, melancholy atmosphere. Only a set of ledger stones tell of the Turner family. Considerably older, ie, thirteenth century, are the arches to tower and chancel. The latter is double-chamfered, the inner on moulded corbels, the outer continuous. The not-too-large tower arch has only a single continuous chamfer. This lovely interior, calm and moving, is one of the most memorable in the whole of East Anglia.

Box pews: 1800-1, as are all the following; plain panelling; stained red.
Chancel panelling: Plain; the south side curved round chancel arch to link up with box pews; an attached bench on south side.
Commandment boards: With depressed-arched tops.
Communion rail: Turned balusters.
Communion table: Heavy turned legs; top with a band of cusped waves, possibly C19.
Font: A lovely stone baluster.
Pulpit (with tester): A three-decker; plain panelling; panelled back-post with volutes; plain tester; book-rests on curly brackets; stairs with turned and square balusters.
South door: With intersecting tracery.
Royal Arms: Of c1820-30; George IV. The Baroque-style chandelier with its pulley is probably C19.
Also four hatchments.

Chislehampton

Chislehampton is one of the best preserved small Georgian village churches in the whole of England, and it and the neighbouring house taken together form an illuminating insight into the social, religious and aesthetic ideals of the eighteenth century. The little chapel-like building, unpretentious and stuccoed, stands alongside the drive of the house, looking as if it were some child's toy rather than a real building. What contrast is represented here between the religious and the secular aspirations of the age — the Church content with a simple preaching house, the Gentry requiring a building which will enhance their status. It is a complete reversal of the medieval situation whereby the rich built and rebuilt churches in preference to providing grand homes for themselves. Chislehampton House was built for Charles Peers, the son of a Lord Mayor of London; he also paid for the church. House and church do not form one group when viewed close by; to see them as such one must travel westwards some distance along the Clifton Hampden road and them look back across the fields.

Chislehampton church was built in 1762, replacing a medieval chapel, and its contents, dating from one stylistic moment, remain essentially in their original condition, a fortuitous survival indeed. The plan is of the utmost simplicity, a single-celled room without any indication of a chancel, an arrangement eminently characteristic of the age. Only the timber bell-turret (disguised to look like stone) strikes a more ambitious note. This consists of two stages, the lower with vermiculated quoins, the upper, open section with pilasters. Below occurs an unusual and very rustic gable, the apex of which is sliced off and replaced by a sunk section springing from miniature volutes. It is probable that this curious feature represents the builder's attempt to design an open scrolly pediment. At the foot of the gable stand two stone urns, and apart from these, a few other stone trimmings, and the light blue door and clock face, everything is of wedding-day whiteness. The windows are plain and round-arched, their only enrichment being a single keystone at the apex. Both north and east walls, however, are devoid of windows. The churchyard is entered between a pair of stone gatepiers, each with a ball on top. Within its borders of neatly-trimmed hedges grow roses, herbaceous plants and an ample spread of lawn. It is all extremely reasonable in intention and effect.

The interior is beautifully preserved. Its impact is immediate and lasting, thanks to the unity of the furnishings, the high standard of craftsmanship, and especially to the fact that one enters from the west. The *ensemble* is thus presented as a symmetrical composition, with the altar framed by the pews and the latter, in turn, framed by the gallery. It is very satisfying and impresses us by its sense of order and classicity, as one would expect, and also by a graphic clarity of detail which runs through architecture, furnishings and monuments alike. Take the architecture, for example. Elaborate details are carefully avoided; instead, clear basic shapes prevail everywhere. The plain arched windows are balanced on the

Interior looking east

Interior looking west

north wall by unenriched blank recesses, with equally plain pilasters flanking each window and recess. A modest dentil cornice travels across at capital level. The pilasters, incidentally, are supported on brackets instead of pedestals, rather a Mannerist conception. A recess of similarly restrained aspects encloses the reredos. This last is the only item among the furnishings which displays a certain elaboration of detail (apart, of course, from the pulpit, which is a century older and belongs to a different epoch). Yet, even here the Rococo garlands do not weaken the bold outline, with its raised broken segmental pediment. This restrained and economic use of form and decoration is the exact antithesis of, for example, Little Stanmore, where profuse enrichment was employed to create Baroque effusiveness. While the latter remains an alien importation of Roman descent, Chislehampton speaks with a quintessentially English voice.

Pulpit: Early C17; a three-decker; pulpit with blank arches and Ionic pilasters at the angles; enriched friezes above and below; the stairs with turned balusters and the reader's and clerk's desks are of 1762.

Box pews: Of 1762, as are all of the following; plain panelling.

Chandeliers: Three of brass; centre one with two tiers of branches, others with a single tier.

Childrens' benches: Flanking the altar.

Communion rail: Three-sided; slender turned balusters.

Font: A plain marble bowl on a wooden pedestal.

Font cover: Square; pyramidal; plain.

Reredos: Tripartite, with a raised broken segmental pediment above the centre flanked by volutes. Rococo garlands of flowers and ribbons. Panels with the Ten Commandments, the Creed and the Lord's Prayer.

West gallery: On slim Tuscan columns; plainly panelled front.

Rycote

Rycote Park and church stand together in an initimate hollow surrounded by trees and approached along a track. The setting is very picturesque, with the red brick gables of the house peering through the trees, the lawns around the church, and the mighty yew near the door. The latter is, of course, far older than any of the buildings. Its trunk is like a titanic piece of sculpture. Tradition says that the tree was planted at the coronation of King Stephen in 1135, a legend that one may or may not believe.

Rycote chapel was built in 1449 by Sir Richard Quatremayne as a chantry endowed with three priests. After Edward VI had dissolved the chantries, the building became the private chapel of a succession of families occupying the house. So it never was a parish church, but is included here because of its remarkable furnishings which survive in a perfect state of preservation. In 1952 the chapel was placed under the guardianship of what is now the Department of the Environment, restored by them, and opened to the public in 1967.

The chapel consists of a nave and chancel in one, dominated by an elegant west tower, ie, it looks, except for the lack of a visible chancel, very much like a small village church. The tower is of three stages and has diagonal buttresses and an embattled parapet, a three-light west window, and a doorway with continuous mouldings. Above the window is a canopied image niche. The bell-openings are similar to the nave windows. The nave-cum-chancel is strongly articulated by buttresses carrying pinnacles. Those at the east corners support chained beasts. The side windows are of two cusped lights under triangular heads, the larger east window of five lights with plain panel tracery. The walls are of stone, the roof of red tiles. Completely unaltered, the exterior offers a rare insight into the kind of building a knight of the county could afford to erect for his own purposes during the late Middle Ages.

Despite this significance, interest is concentrated inside. It is an uniquely lovely interior, cool and monumental, and with a feeling of time suspended, due in part, no doubt, to the knowledge that the building is really a museum piece now. Yet the furnishings are so perfect, and so untouched by any changes after about 1700, that one can almost visualize the Norreyses sitting in their pew and the estate workers in the benches down below. The pew on the south side, with its ogee canopy, is said to have been erected for a visit of Charles I in 1625, but as it originally carried a statue of the Virgin and Child, it may preferably be assigned to the 1630s, ie, the time of Laud. These two pews, standing opposite one another, appear to close off the chancel from the centre of activity and reduce

Interior from the gallery

The sanctuary

the altar to a distant irrelevance. They reinforce the pulpit's prime function as the liturgical focus, an arrangement eminently characteristic of our 'prayer-book' epoch. This would have been more noticeable before the first Earl of Abingdon re-equipped the chancel in 1682, for the original reredos, now kept under the tower, is insignificant compared with the later one. The distinguished floor of black-and-white marble is his, too. Old red tiles cover the nave floor. The continuous fifteenth-century roof is quite striking in its evenness and consistency. It is a pointed wagon roof with thin purlins, and a section at the west end has had its seventeenth-century decoration restored. This consists of stars on blue fields and also imitation marbling. The tower arch has a broad continuous hollow and one order of shafts, but is partly concealed by the gallery.

Screen and family pew

Font: C12 bowl, C15 stem; plain circular bowl; octagonal panelled stem.

Benches: c1449; straight-topped ends with buttress-shafts.

Font cover: c1449; ribbed ogee dome with finial.

Stalls: c1449; ends with poppyheads; fonts with blank tracery.

Family pew: Early C17; round-arched arcading with Tuscan balusters, lead spandrels and dentils; ceiling with stars and clouds; upper gallery with elaborate pierced filigree panels and Ionic angle pilasters with arabesque.

Pulpit (with tester): Early C17; a two-decker; square pulpit with paired blank arches in arabesque frames; also lozenges; back-post as pulpit; square tester with panelling on underside and also arabesque; the reader's desk with plain panelling is C18.

Screen: Early C17; with a strapwork cresting.

West gallery: Early C17; on wooden Ionic columns painted black to simulate touch (a type of black marble); the pedestals with baluster motifs; balustraded front with turned balusters and dentils; ceiling with stars and clouds.

Former reredos: 1610; attached Ionic columns carrying round arches; leaf spandrels; Ten Commandments.

Family pew: c1630; arcading as before but in two storeys; ogee canopy with crocketed ribs, guilloche cornice, two standing allegorical figures, and ribs inside with a thistle boss; painted stars.

Communion rail: 1682; twisted balusters.

Reredos: 1682; tripartite; open and broken segmental pediment on Corinthian columns enclosing a coat of arms; leaf friezes; Ten Commandments in round-arched frames with leaf borders and segmental pediments; Lord's Prayer and Creed in rectangular frames as above but with triangular pediments; outer Corinthian columns.

Wheatfield

Wheatfield is a melancholy sight now. The little church, with its lovely cream to orange rendering, stands alone in the park, looking westwards across level grassland where once a mansion stood. The churchyard, now rough and neglected, is surrounded by iron railings going to pieces, and they, in turn, are paralleled by a barbed wire fence, such an unwelcome intrusion. Yet the interior, as we shall see, is not in the least neglected, and the low-lying stables further west have been converted into homes. The park, too, is especially beautiful, with its views northwards over a lake and away into distant Oxfordshire. A spindly yew by the west front of the church provides effective textural contrast with the rendered walls.

The east wall of the church presents to the approaching visitor a typical and loveable Georgian paradox. The east window is correctly Venetian, ie, is Classical, but the gable above has a frill of sweet Gothick battlements. This playful juxtaposition continues throughout the building. So the first impression is that of an eighteenth-century church, but the building, in effect, is medieval in its bones, and will be recognised as such from blocked doorways and windows which occur here and there. Wheatfield House was purchased by the Rudge family in 1727 and rebuilt by them, as also was the church. The actual dates are not known. A fire destroyed the house in 1814. The church consists of a nave with bell-turret and west porch, and a slightly narrower chancel. The blocked north and south doorways are fourteenth century, but whether they represent a church newly-built then, or an earlier one rebuilt, cannot be ascertained. They have continuous

mouldings. There is also a blocked fifteenth-century window in the chancel wall. Everything else is of the eighteenth century. The west porch has a pediment and the minimal bell-turret is of timber and lead and sports an ogee dome. The side windows are plain round-arched lights with keystone and clear glass. Above, the same Gothick battlements as those of the gables run along. The Venetian east window has its lights separated by unfluted Ionic columns. There are also outer Ionic pilasters, and everything is enhanced by lichens. What is the date of the Georgian work? If the house was rebuilt about 1730, the church may have followed about 1740, and that would accord well with the Kentian Gothick of the battlements.

The interior is perfectly preserved and is characterised by an all-pervading orange glow which emanates from the chocolate-orange-cream colouring of the walls. Dark brown furnishings provide an effective contrast. The iron chandeliers contain real candles, and there are, indeed, no modern fittings to spoil this period *ensemble*. The chancel is surprisingly spacious and quite stately in the way that it is raised a little above the level of the nave. As with so many Georgian churches which display Gothick motifs in their architecture, Wheatfield's furnishings are unequivocally of Classical design. They prove that the Gothick is purely a Romantic allusion. The pews in the chancel, and also the communion rail, have been stripped of their varnish. Their natural surfaces appeal today for the same reason that makes us prefer the bare texture of medieval stone carving to the original highly-

Communion table: detail

Family pew: detail

coloured effect. The chancel arch is fourteenth century, single-chamfered, and with moulded capitals. It appears to have been cut back during the eighteenth-century reconstruction. The ceiled roof has its tie-beams, octagonal kingposts and four-way struts exposed. The relative thinness of the members suggests a seventeenth-century date.

All furnishings are of c1740.
Box pews: Plain panelling; some have hat pegs.
Chancel pews: As box pews.
Communion rail: Twisted balusters and panelled newels.
Communion Table: Cabriole legs with leaf decoration; top with cherubs' heads, grapes and wheat, and a band of Greek key.
Family pew: Large, with pierced leaf scrolls.
Font: Urn-shaped; fluted bowl on a bulbous stem.
Font cover: Flat; central moulded finial.
Pulpit (with tester): A two-decker; tall plain panels and also leaf friezes; thin back-post; tester with leaf and simple inlay.
Royal Arms: 1742; of George II.
Stained glass: Arms of the Rudge family in west window.
Text boards: Ten Commandments, Lord's Prayer and Creed.
Wall panelling: Around the font; plain. Also one hatchment.

Widford

Exterior from the south-west

Box pews and wall painting

Widford church stands upon sloping ground above the picturesquely-named River Windrush, immediately adjacent to where it broadens into a shallow pool, its soggy banks deep-pitted by the hooves of wallowing cattle. A few ragged elms and a number of twisted and stunted hawthorns keep company with the building, which is otherwise isolated, approachable only along footpaths. Therein lies one facet of its appeal; another is its ability to blend with its surroundings, a complement to the natural features of the site. A further distinction is its utter simplicity and unpretentiousness.

The church, of a barn-like austerity, is, from the foundations to the tip of the bellcote, constructed entirely of stone, and the encircling churchyard wall is of the same material. So are several walls in the adjoining fields, providing continuity of texture and character. The basic cubes of nave and chancel are capped by an elementary triangular roof shape, and this combination is repeated at right-angles, and in a vertical plane, in the bellcote placed mid-way along the roof. The windows, which are nearly all straight-headed, also take part in this general rectangularity. Such simple means, characteristic of good vernacular building, are also employed in the churchyard, which is nothing more than an extension of the surrounding field, defined only by its drystone wall. Field and churchyard thus flow into each other, and the whole is as unassuming as a village pound.

Widford is a thirteenth-century church untouched by any subsequent major alterations. The plan consists of a nave and chancel, undivided externally except by the afore-mentioned bellcote. Original single trefoiled lancets survive in the chancel, but the east window is a nineteenth-century replacement with reticulated tracery. It does no harm. The nave, conversely, displays a medley of Perpendicular and post-Reformation windows. The former can be seen in the south wall; just two single, straight-headed lights. The west and north windows are either late sixteenth or early seventeenth century and are, with their plain mullioned and transomed lights, unashamedly domestic.

This unaffected character continues inside, and it is a salutary thought to realise, in an age of gimmicky and contrived design, how superior unconscious artistry can be. Perhaps the essential quality is an unswerving integrity of design and an honest use of the materials involved. The chancel arch, for example, is a purely functional opening into the chancel, for elaboration would be superfluous here. The box pews express in a profoundly uncomplicated way their true purpose, that of providing draught-proof seating for the congregation. Decorative enrichment would detract from their eloquent utility. Simplicity is, indeed, the hallmark of this interior, with its homely whitewashed walls, the floor flagged with stones, the atmosphere perfumed by freshly cut flowers. The windows are leaded with small diamond panes or quarries, especially noticeable here because nothing, except the wall paintings exposed in great jagged patches, competes with their strong repetitive patterns. In the chancel, which is happily uncluttered, is a whole series of paintings and, most memorable of all, two sections of a Roman mosaic pavement preserved *in situ*. The continuity expressed by these latter fragments is truly unforgettable, and here, in this remote Oxfordshire valley, we can recognize a symbolic manifestation of Christianity's triumph over Pagan Rome.

We have talked about integrity of design and honesty in the employment of materials, and have referred to features which satisfactorily express these concepts. Yet when the visitor turns to the communion table he will be confronted with an object, pleasing as it is in itself, which does not reflect a desire to

Communion rail and table

conform to such reasonable objectives. For this table is neo-Jacobean, ie, is a period imitation. The decision to employ a past style was made, no doubt, out of a genuine wish to 'keep in keeping', but the essential point has been missed. Take any of the old furnishings, the fifteenth-century pulpit, the Jacobean communion rail, the Regency box pews, and it will be noted that each is a product of its own time and of one stylistic moment. Compromises with the past have been eschewed. So why make concessions now? Surely a suitable table of modern design would not detract from the charms of this little building? Or is it that modern glass-and-concrete has forced us not to trust our own aesthetic sensibilities? It is with this worrying thought that we take our leave of Widford.

Font: C13; tub-shaped and plain.
Wall paintings: C14; in the chancel; two tiers on each side; the Living and the Dead Kings; a martyrdom; saints.
Wall paintings: C15; in the nave; St Christopher, partly obliterated by a C17 royal arms.
Pulpit: C15; of wood; polygonal; with simple traceried panelling.
Communion rail: Early C17; dumb-bell balusters.
Commandment boards: C17; the usual texts.
Box pews: Early C19; plain panelling; the higher squire's pew on the right.

Brooke

The church forms the centrepiece of a splendidly rural architectural group, with flanking brick and stone cottages, the whole looking as if it had been set out by an improving squire. Yet it is, of course, entirely fortuitous, and being so achieves without effort the visual success that we today so consciously and unsuccessfully strive for. The verges and banks are rough and tangled, not tamed and suburbanised in the way that some best-kept-village fanatics would have it. The churchyard, with a good selection of lichened headstones, is entered through a simple iron gate guarded by the most delightful of Victorian lamps. It is exactly the same type as one used to find on country railway stations.

The west view of the church is happily idiosyncratic, with splendid contrasts of form. The solid-looking, four-square tower appears to taper outwards towards the top, and is balanced by the lower, sharply-pointed gable of the north aisle. This, in turn, has a little, asymmetrically-placed chimney stack sprouting wild plants. There is also a textural contrast between the random stonework of the tower and the ashlaring of the aisle. The church is entirely built of stone, the nave of ironstone, the roofs of stone slates. The plan is a parallelogram, with nave and chancel to the south, aisle and chapel to the north. Only the west tower and south porch break this longitudinal clarity.

The original church dated from the twelfth century and consisted of a nave, a chancel and, to anticipate the arcade inside, a north aisle. Of all this only the south doorway tells externally. It has an arch, made pointed later on, with right-angle chevron forming lozenges and an inner roll, square abaci, and one order of shafts without any capitals. The date is about 1160, but some alterations have obviously been made. To this church a tower was added in the thirteenth century. It is of three diminishing stages and has an embattled parapet on corbels and a west window in the form of a single lancet. The bell-openings consist of two lights with a middle shaft, set within a larger arch on nook-shafts. The shafts carry leaf capitals, and the area above the paired lights is solid, ie, is just pre-plate tracery and can thus be assigned to about 1240. Of the

Family pews and benches

fifteenth century there is just one window in the nave south wall, the one with four cusped lights and a straight hood-mould on head stops.

Despite the visual predominance of the tower, the external character is largely determined by the work of about 1579 in a Gothic Survival vein. The porch is of that time and has a round-arched doorway with plain responds. But the major elements of that Elizabethan campaign are the north aisle and chancel, rebuilt from pre-existing structures, and an added north chapel. They are characterised by three and four light mullioned windows with round-arched lights and straight hood-moulds. There also occur two such windows in the nave south wall. The mullions here are hollow-chamfered, but in the aisle they are moulded instead. The west window of the aisle has a window with two plain square-headed lights, entirely domestic. This 'debased' Perpendicular is typical of the age and contrasts tellingly with the proud Revivalism of Staunton Harold.

Upon entering the church do not overlook the sinister, centipede-like hinges on the back of the north door opposite. They form a diversion from the tranquillity of this spacious,

Communion rail and table

amply lit and fully furnished interior. It is an interior different from most in this book in the sense that the usual 'prayer-book' concentration of furnishings is absent. The individual elements which one expects to find are, of course, all there, but they are more diffused owing to the larger area to be filled. The east end, in any case, is singularly devoid of furnishings, the chapel especially so, but this allows the architectural spaces to speak with added force. The importance of this interior lies essentially in the complete survival of its furnishings datable to about 1579, the only such set from the late sixteenth century in the country, and perhaps the earliest following the Elizabethan Settlement. The furnishings are remarkably consistent and harmonize well with the architecture. As regards the latter, details are as follows. The three-bay north arcade takes us back to the mid-twelfth century. It has round single-chamfered arches, square abaci, circular piers and enriched volute capitals. Then comes the thirteenth-century tower arch, triple-stepped and chamfered, with two orders of shafts carrying, possibly uncut, moulded capitals.

The north chapel arcade is of about 1579 with two bays of round moulded arches, square chamfered piers, and moulded capitals caught in a stylistic limbo between moulded-medieval and Tuscan-Classical. The chancel and chapel west arches are identical. Of about 1579 also are the roofs, except possibly for that of the chancel which may be recent. This is of the arched-braced type whereas the others have cambered tie-beams and moulded purlins. The floors are entirely of stone.

Font: C12; square; blank arches on colonnettes with leaf capitals. All other furnishings are of c1579.
Benches: Plain ends with blocky poppyheads.
Box pews: Plain panelling; higher backs with bands of hoop-like decoration.
Chancel screen: Plain panelling; decoration as box pews; turned balusters.
Communion rail: Two-sided; strong vertically symmetrical turned balusters.
Communion table: Heavy turned legs; marble top.
Communion table: In the chapel; turned legs.
Family pew: On north side; plain panelling; decoration as box pews; balustrade with turned balusters.
Family pew: On south side; as above but with solid panels between the balusters with horizontal pierced panels containing lozenges in rectangles.
Font cover: Square; pyramidal; tall leaf finial.
North chapel screen: Plain panelling; turned balusters.
North chapel west screen: Ditto.
Pulpit (with tester): Plain panelling; book-rest on curly brackets; plainly panelled back-post; tester with pendants and dentils.
Reader's desk: As upper half of south family pew: band of guilloche; knobs.
Stalls: Plain panelling; backs with a frieze of arabesque leaf; ends as benches.
Tower screen: As chancel screen but with thicker balusters.

Heath

There are not many unaltered Norman village churches in England; not even Iffley, to name one famous twelfth-century building. Yet Heath is just that, belonging to a select band which includes, for instance, Kilpeck in Herefordshire and Stewkley in Buckinghamshire. In addition, our Shropshire church scores over nearly all of them in that it preserves a complete 'prayer-book' interior. Its closest parallel is thus Winterborne Tomson in Dorset, yet the setting and character of each church differs markedly. At Heath, the architecture asserts itself in its own right, while at Winterborne it appears to be merely a frame, a *mise-en-scène*, for the furnishings. Heath stands entirely alone, pat in the middle of a field, the site of a deserted medieval village, a field neatly maintained by the occasional visitation of a flock of sheep. There is not even a footpath to the door, let alone a proper churchyard. It is a setting that suits the stern Norman elevations to perfection.

The church consists of a nave and slightly smaller chancel; that is all, and the visitor will look in vain for a bell-turret, porch, or any other protuberance. The builders chose their stone carefully. While the walls are of a greyish to pink sandstone, buttresses, doorway, etc, are picked out in a yellower stone. It is a lovely effect. The west wall displays a trio of strong, flat buttresses linked at waist level by a string-course which, incidentally, runs all the way round. The four windows are narrow, round-headed lancets, one being set into the middle buttress, the others forming a stepped tripartite group under the gable. Identical windows and buttresses occur everywhere, the windows being remarkably small and undemonstrative. The east wall is similar to the west front but has only the one window in the centre. Only the south doorway attempts something more in the way of enrichment. Its arch has an inner roll and an outer band of chevron, and there is also right-angle chevron in the soffits. The hood-mould also has chevron. The two orders of shafts, of a greyer stone, carry decayed scalloped capitals, and there is, in addition, a plain tympanum. From the occurrence of chevron placed at right-angles to the wall plane, one may assign the church to about 1150-60. Finally, there exists just one later feature, the seventeenth-century nave north-east window, a plain square light with a wooden casement.

Inside, the Norman ruggedness continues and seemingly penetrates even the furnishings. The absence of elegance and finesse appears to reflect the straightforward, rough-and-ready character of the Normans themselves. It is a surprisingly well-lit interior, considering the minuteness of the windows as they appeared outside. Perhaps the deep splays help to spread the light. The walls have a coating of old, flaking plaster that displays a fine medley of colour; white, greys, creams, and the faint ghosts of wall paintings all intertwined. The stone floor varies from dark grey to fawn. The chancel arch has three plain, stepped orders, and two orders of nook-shafts carrying scalloped capitals. The details are much simpler than those of the doorway, indicating that the latter formed the end of the building campaign. What is the date of the roofs? Their tie-beams and struts look extremely old; perhaps the thirteenth century is the answer. Their homely rusticity reflects that of

Exterior from the south-west

the furnishings, and it is for this special quality that one will remember the interior, just as one will remember the architecture for its remarkable completeness.

Font: C12; circular; tub-shaped; a band of incised arches around the top; square base set diagonally.

South door: C12; the hinges with C-shaped scrolls.

Benches: Late C15(?); straight-topped ends with vertical grooving.

Bench: C17, as are all the following; in the chancel; incorporating a medieval newel post with a strange finial shaped like an unfolding flower.

Box pews: Plain panelling; one pew in the chancel incorporates C15 bench ends (one with a circle of tracery) and the base or top of a screen with crenellation.

Communion rail: Three-sided; slim turned balusters.

Communion table: With slim turned legs.

Pulpit: a two-decker; upper tier of panelling with rosettes in lozenges.

Squire's pew: As box pews but with panelling as pulpit.

Interior looking west

Interior looking east

Langley

The little chapel stands all alone in a large field of lush grass, with only cows for company. The setting is elevated and breezy, the hilly horizons shrouded in woodland. All that is left of Langley Hall, the gatehouse, lies in a hollow some way further to the east. It is a curious experience to come upon the solitary chapel in these quiet pastoral hills. Its forms are surprisingly large-scaled for so small a building, the elevations clearly outlined, the details never fussy. The walls are of a yellowish to greenish sandstone ashlar, and the roof is covered with stone slates.

The building consists of a single-celled nave-cum-chancel, with an ample bell-turret above the west gable. The turret is weatherboarded, and has rectangular, louvred lights and a pyramid cap. There are two doorways in the south wall, one, the main doorway, with a segmental arch, the other, the priest's entrance, with a Tudor arch. They both have single chamfers. The chancel has diagonal buttresses of one set-off. In the nave

north wall is a plain, rectangular, two-light, mullioned window; its opposite number on the south side is a single, plain, round-arched light. The west window is a single lancet, and that leaves only the chancel east window which is of a different order altogether. It is a large arched window with three stepped lights set in, and so is of a familiar late thirteenth-century Herefordshire/Shropshire type. The mullions, characteristically, are carried right up against the main arch. This window brings us to the question of dates. Two exist; 1564 and 1601. The former appears outside, the latter inside on a roof beam. 1601 seems the more likely, though 1564 cannot be ruled out. The west window supports the later date; one would expect something more debased-Perpendicular from a decade not too distant in time from the Reformation. As for the east window, could it not be an eighteenth-century replacement? If it is 1601, it is an early case of Gothic Revivalism, though one must not overlook certain medievalizing tendencies at the beginning of the seventeenth century (eg Lulworth Castle, Dorset, of about 1608). Unless further documentary evidence comes to light, it is unlikely that the matter will be resolved.

The interior is very moving in its Puritan way. In fact, it is as stark and uncompromising as King's Norton, though of a very different kind. The concrete floor of the nave, while not attractive in itself, reinforces the austere effect. The floor at the east end, on the other hand, is covered with medieval tiles.

Exterior from the south-west

The sanctuary

They are mainly red and blue, with tracery designs and shields. They provide the sole relief in an interior almost entirely white and brown. The arrangement at the east end is of great interest, being almost unique (cf Hailes). The communion table stands forward away from the wall and is surrounded by a three-sided rail placed back-to-front, as it were, so that the transverse bar is behind the table. It is an extreme Puritan plan and one must be thankful for its survival. The table is a modern reproduction. Elsewhere I have argued that new additions to churches ought to be in a contemporary style, but here at Langley period imitation seems justified for several reasons. Firstly, all the furnishings are of a piece, none being later than about 1601. Secondly, the chapel is virtually a museum piece; it has never served as a parish church, and only very occasionally are services held here. Thirdly, the original table was stolen a few years ago! Another rare survival is the movable pulpit; it is the only example among our fifty churches.

The chancel roof is single-framed and has collars on straight braces. That of the nave has tie-beams, collars on arched braces, and wind-braces. The braces rest upon corbels with, variously, heads, fleurs-de-lis and steps. At the west end is the framework for the bell-turret, with simple braces, etc. It is open right to the very top, creating an unexpected spacial digression. On the south side of the nave the wall is extended up between the beams and is enriched with rosettes and fleurs-de-lis executed in plaster. This perfect post-Reformation chapel is now under the guardianship of the Department of the Environment.

All furnishings are of c1601 or 1564.
Benches: Plain ends with poppyheads like lollipops.
Box pews: Plain panelling; top frieze of straight-sided ovals; knobs.
Communion rail: Three-sided; plain bench top with book-rest and boards for kneeling.
Musicians' pew: At the west end; as box pews but open.
Pulpit: Free-standing and movable; panelling, etc, as box pews.
Reader's desk: Large and square; as box pews; flat canopy on two upper sides; beautiful tiger-skin graining.
The replacement communion table dates from 1969.

Langley: *Reader's desk: detail*

Hardington

Hardington is a hamlet of farm buildings on the eastern flank of the Mendips, a seemingly remote spot, yet one not more than four miles from Radstock. The church lies tucked away behind the farm and nestles in a tight-fitting churchyard surrounded by high hedges and numerous trees. The churchyard is open to the east and separated from the adjoining house by nothing more than a rickety railing. A monkey-puzzle tree, always a thrilling sight, guards both house and church. This quiet, reflective corner of Somerset is spoilt by the modern farm buildings that stand just to the north. Always ugly, they appear even more cruel and hard here when contrasted against the lovely textured surfaces of the church.

The church, at first sight, appears larger than it really is, due, no doubt, to the closeness of the hedges. Yet it is quite a small building, having only a nave and chancel and a miniature west tower, the latter looking more like a bellcote when viewed from the east. Chancel and tower are ashlar-faced, the nave is of random stone, and the east wall is spattered with lichens. The roofs are of stone slates. The church seems to have been built anew during the early fourteenth century; nothing older survives, unless the nave walls represent an earlier structure. Of early fourteenth-century details we have the following. There are a pair of two-light windows in both the north and south walls of the nave, with cinquecusped ogee lights, a reticulation unit in the head, and hood-moulds on head-stops. The buttresses here are probably coeval, but have been recut in recent times. Their interesting profiles, with the keeled set-offs, are no doubt more elaborate than the original ones would have been. The chancel window is of the three-stepped-lights under-one-arch type, with inset trefoiled sub-arches and a hood-mould on big leaf stops. It is obviously Victorian in its present state; the hardness tells. Was the early fourteenth-century original identical, or is this a Middle-Pointed revision? Only an old drawing could provide the answer.

The tower was added in the late fifteenth century, a tiny structure whose smallness of scale will be more readily appreciated inside. It is divided into two stages and has a splendid crown which consists of a bold embattled parapet, tall crocketed pinnacles, and appealing gargoyles. The latter include a man holding a mask, a monkey doing the same, and two monsters' heads. The bell-openings are plain, single, uncusped lights set in rectangular frames, the west window a small, similar, but cusped light. Above is an image niche with a nodding canopy under ogee gables, crocketed pinnacles, and triangular buttress-shafts. New windows were inserted in the chancel side walls during the early sixteenth century; their plain, round-arched lights under a straight hood-mould are typical of the time of Henry VIII. The south doorway is early eighteenth century, round-arched and chamfered, and with block-like keystone and abaci.

The interior is one of the loveliest in the west, sparsely furnished, bathed in light, and of the utmost simplicity and meaningfulness. At the time of writing, it is being restored by the Redundant Churches Fund who now maintain the church. Their loving, caring hand is apparent for all to see in the redecoration of the chancel. The nave walls still display the old plaster surfaces with their patchwork of browns, creams and

The exterior

greys. The stone floors possess a greyish tinge. Near the door, and hidden among the pews, is an ogee-arched piscina; it proves the existence of a nave altar here. The chancel arch present a problem for the historian trying to establish dates. Pevsner says it is not medieval. At first glance, the plain, single-stepped, round arch, the hacked-off square abaci, and the battered scalloped capitals left over from the long-vanished nook-shafts, all look genuinely Norman, ie, early twelfth century. It cannot be Victorian, nor of the previous two centuries. In any case, who would want to erect a sham Norman arch in such a place? Some modification to accommodate a rood screen during the fifteenth century would account for the maltreatment. If it is authentic, as it seems to be, it pushes the origins of the building back by two hundred years. The tiny tower arch, more like a doorway than a full-blown arch, presents no problems. It has a depressed arch and is late fifteenth century. The fourteenth-century nave roof is a flattened wagon roof with moulded beams, leaf bosses at the intersections, and a wall plate with moulded corbels. The chancel roof is flat and ceiled.

Font: C12; square bowl with lunette sides curving under to the stem; circular stem; moulded base.
Royal Arms: 1640; of Charles I. The remaining furnishings are late C18-early C19.
Box pews: Plain panelling; the slightly taller pew opposite the pulpit was probably the squire's.
Communion rail: Slim turned balusters; the rail curves up concavely either end.

Box pews and pulpit

Communion table: Heavy twisted legs; a lion's head at each corner; band of incised leaf.

Font cover; Square; concave sides rising to a flat finial.
Pulpit: A three-decker; plain panelling; panelled angle pilasters; reader's and clerk's desks part of box pews.

114

Sheaves of corn in the nave

Ingestre

Ingestre is a strangely remote place. The lane leading to it dissolves into an unmetalled track here and there, and reminds one of how isolated such villages were before the onslaught of the motor age. Interest is concentrated on the house, or rather for our purposes, the church, and its surroundings. House, church and accessory buildings form a splendid set of architectural sequences and are reached along, yet again, a

rutted driveway which seems openly hostile to the passage of a car. The group unfolds slowly; first one passes the mighty and ruinous nineteenth-century stables on the left, then the earlier former stables on the right. After that one rounds a corner and then the house appears in line ahead, with the church on one side, the park on the other. Nothing disturbs this peaceful *ensemble* except for the infrequent car proceeding to the house, now a college. It all seems so very far removed from the transitory and illusionary world of industrial England.

Ingestre church was designed, it seems, by Sir Christopher Wren and built in 1676. It is the first fully Classical church outside the City of London and Wren's only provincial ecclesiastical building. Walter Chetwynd, who owned the hall, was a member of the Royal Society, as was Wren. The great architect produced a drawing labelled 'Mr Chetwynd's tower', but this does not specifically refer to the church. However, the quality of the church and the existence of the drawing are too coincidental. In any case, who else but Wren was capable of designing such a church at that time? Certainly not Robert Hooke; his church at Willen, Buckinghamshire, of 1679, is much too derivative. That leaves Henry Bell, who began his All Saints, Northampton also in 1676. True, that is essentially a Classical design, but it displays several Gothic and other quirks absent at Ingestre. The quality of Ingestre's interior also speaks of Wren.

The building consists of a west tower, a nave with aisles and clerestory, and a chancel. The material is a greyish-yellow ashlar. The tower has three unequal stages, the lower with alternating quoins, the others with unstressed corners. This ground stage has a doorway framed by Tuscan columns carrying a pediment. A coat of arms sits upon the pediment, and the doorway has plain Tuscan pilasters. The round-arched bell-openings have plain frames, the parapet a balustrade with urns. In the narrow middle stage occur, to north and south, circular windows, and they effectively link the tower to the body of the church. It is a much more successful solution to the problem of joining tower to nave than Gibbs was to employ later at St Martin-in-the-Fields. The windows and aisles and chancel are identical, being large and round-arched, and set in slight projections. They have leaf volute keystones which link up with the cornice above. The east window of the chancel is odd and unexpected. It is not the usual Venetian type but consists, instead, of three individual stepped lights separated by volute corbels. Another such volute occurs above the centre light. Does one detect the hand of a local builder here? There is an open pediment above this group.

The visitor enters the church via a circular lobby. He will be confronted by a majestic interior of rich grandeur, an interior as urbane and harmonious as anything in London. It is completely unaltered, too, which is more than one can say for Wren's City churches. Only the nineteenth-century glass in the east window detracts. The only other major Classical church that can rival it in authenticity is Wanstead, Essex, of a hundred years later. Of the furnishings, the screen and pulpit

Nave ceiling: detail

Pulpit: detail

are fully worthy of Wren and up to the best standards of the City churches. The joiners and carvers are not known. The four-bay arcades have round arches with heads as keystones, and the piers are in the form of four engaged Tuscan demi-columns carrying square entablature sections. There is a moulded cornice immediately above the arches. The chancel is similar but has plain responds. The tower arch is blank and has an inset doorway. The clerestory windows are not enriched inside. The flat nave ceiling is exquisitely decorated. It has a wide central oval with leaf border, the spandrels with garlands emerging from vases. At the east and west cardinal points occur cherubs' heads with lovely stylized wings. The rectangular end panels, with their inturned corners, display the most delicately undercut leaf borders and fronds placed crossed-sword-wise. There are also trails of leaf whorls and the cornice has festoons. The tunnel vaulted chancel is quieter. It is divided into nine panels, the centre emphasised by an acanthus frame and a coat of arms. The other panels contain shields in leaf borders and the cornice is enriched by leafy modillions and egg-and-dart. As usual, the chancel has a floor of black-and-white marble arranged in squares and also squares of triangles. The nave and aisles have stone floors.

Can the motifs at Ingestre be paralleled with those employed by Wren elsewhere? Clerestories he often used (eg, St Bride 1671-8); circular clerestory windows more rarely (eg St Martin Ludgate 1677-84). The type of tower with balustrade and urns recurs at St Andrew Holborn, of 1684-90, the unadorned, round-arched bell-openings at St Magnus (1671-6). As for the Tuscan order of the doorway, Wren used this most effectively at Trinity College library, Cambridge (begun 1676). The longitudinal plan with nave, aisles and arcades in the medieval way can be seen at, again, St Bride. St Margaret Pattens (1684-7) has a flat ceiling. The closest parallel to the arcade piers, with their four attached Tuscan columns, is St Bride, once more. But there the piers have only two columns paired in depth. They carry the same square entablature sections.

All furnishings are of c1676.
Box pews: Plain panelling.
Chancel panelling: Panels with shouldered tops and acanthus borders separated by garlands suspended from cherubs' heads; acanthus friezes.
Communion rail: Three-sided; also north and south extensions; turned balusters with Ionic capitals.
Communion table: Twisted legs with Ionic capitals.
Font: An enriched marble baluster; gadrooned bowl; acanthus at the foot.
Font cover: Circular; flat; acanthus leaves curling up against a pineapple finial.
Nave panelling: Plain; also panelling around the pier bases.
Pulpit (with tester): A two-decker; pulpit panels with enriched frames set within borders of garlands with cherubs' heads; stairs with wrought-iron rails including S-shaped motifs; back-post panelled as above but with drapes and a curly open pediment; tester with leaf friezes and a central leaf pendant; reader's desk with leaf volutes.
Screen: Three arches divided by Corinthian pilasters, the arches on further pilasters; cherubs' heads in spandrels; garlands and festoons; pierced leaf panels below and in gates; cresting with the Royal Arms.

Letheringham

Monastic ruins often arouse the strongest imaginative responses in those who wander at leisure among their sad, haunting fragments. One can fully appreciate why they appealed so greatly to the Picturesque writers of the late eighteenth century. And, though we, in our archaeologically and historically more accurate age, no longer relish in such phrases as 'awful arches that make a solemn noonday light', the aura of mystery, the sense of things unseen but seeing, nonetheless remains. Thus it is at Letheringham, for the church is a fragment of an Augustinian priory founded about 1200, and the fifteenth-century brick gatehouse, the only other surviving building, stands in an adjacent field. The churchyard is surprisingly spacious, tangled and surrounded by a brick wall. The dark line of trees to the south effectively enhances the Romantic atmosphere of this brooding, time-worn place.

The church consists of a west tower and a nave with south porch; the chancel was demolished about 1789. No doubt the whole building is of flint, but the nave is rendered. Only the porch does not conform; it is of red brick instead. The roof is of red tiles. It is a pretty building, despite the loss of the east parts. The architectural story begins in the twelfth century with the south doorway. This had an arch with a band of chevron and two rolls, the inner continuous. There are also nook-shafts carrying scalloped capitals and a hood-mould with billet. Judging by the extant details, the whole church, including the chancel, was rebuilt about 1300. The windows, two south, one east, have intersecting tracery, uncusped to the south, cusped to the east. The latter is the former chancel east window re-set. The north side is devoid of windows. The tower was added about 1320. It has slender, flushwork-panelled, diagonal buttresses and an embattled parapet with stepped merlons, again flushwork, and minimal pinnacles. The bell-openings, and also the main west window, have reticulated tracery. The dear little porch dates from 1685. It sports a somewhat eccentrically shaped gable with a straight-sided upper section on convex shanks. The doorway is round-arched, and there is also a small round-arched side light with a wooden mullion.

The interior displays an air of adaptation, as one would expect of a church that has been the victim of so many vicissitudes. This process began even before the Dissolution, for the Decorated tower arch incorporates Norman fragments probably from a former west doorway. They, like the south doorway, pre-date the foundation of the priory, which must have annexed a parish church. The arch is dramatically tall for so small a church; it has one roll and thin, stove-pipe nook-shafts carrying small scalloped capitals. There are also fragments of a chevron band. The late eighteenth century did more; a neat sanctuary was created against the new east wall, the roof was ceiled, and new furnishings introduced. The pair of kneeling figures from a Jacobean monument may also have been placed in their niches at this time. The floor is a melange of

Exterior from the south-east

Lamp bracket

yellow bricks, inset brasses, and ledger stones. The present century has been less kind in its desire to provide modern comforts for the congregation. While the simple lighting arrangement does no harm, the electric heaters clamped onto the walls, and connected to each other by orange cable, are antipathetic in the extreme. How can incumbents be so impervious towards the visual sensibilities of their churches?

Font: C12; plain circular bowl and stem; square base.
Benches: C17; plain ends with wavy tops. All other furnishings are probably of c1789.
Box pews: plain panelling.
Communion rail: Three-sided; slender turned balusters.
Font cover: Circular; eight-sided; rising concavely to a plain finial.
Lamp brackets: Of wrought-iron; horizontal arm on scrolls.
Pulpit: A two-decker; plain panelling.
Reader's desk: Separate, like a lectern; turned balusters.
Royal Arms: Of George III.
Wall panelling: Plain; behind box pews only.
The communion table is modern.

Ledger stone

Shelland

The tree-shrouded churchyard forms a barrier between two contrasting visual worlds. To the north there is commonland backed by distant cottages, a spacious scene of rural habitation of the kind one finds in paintings by Leader. Walk through the churchyard and before you stretches an expansive field dipping gently to far-off hedgerows. At the time of our visit, the field was a vast sea of beet. The little church is easily

Exterior from the south

Interior looking west

outstripped by the surrounding trees; many exceed its modest dimensions in both height and girth. The exterior is rendered and demure, yet full of inimitable charm. The churchyard, characterised by a good collection of wavy-topped headstones, is entered through natural arches of evergreens.

The church has a nave with a bell-turret placed astride a steeply pitched roof, and a much lower chancel. A north porch is balanced on the south side by a vestry. The rendering has been scored to resemble ashlar; the roofs are of red tiles. The building was erected in 1767 but some of the windows, it seems, were altered later. The bell-turret is also rendered and has a lead ogee canopy with a ball finial. Indicative of the date are the bell-openings with the slight ogee tips to their otherwise plain arches. The porch has a doorway with the brickwork exposed. It has chamfers and quadrant demi-shafts carrying

Chancel and communion rails

moulded capitals. The doorway inside is plainly chamfered. Above it occurs a rough cherub's head. The vestry opposite has a plain arched window with Y-tracery glazing bars, probably a later insertion. The walls here are corbelled out to meet the gable and this motif is repeated throughout the church. The west window is a bold quarterfoiled circle, the two westernmost windows on each side single, attenuated lancets. These are of 1767 but the others further east, ie, those with Y-tracery, must be of the late eighteenth or the early nineteenth century. Definitely early nineteenth century is the chancel east window, with its ogee lights and plain panel tracery.

The interior is one of the most endearing anywhere and will weave its spell around the heart of all but the most indifferent visitor. Not only are the furnishings perfectly preserved, but certain eccentricities occur which seem unique to Shelland and bring a retrospective smile to anyone who has paid a visit here. The chancel, for example, is partly fabric-covered; there is a crazy colour scheme; and the nave is watched over by a sweet Gothick organ raised high up on the former musicians' pew. The arrangement of the furnishings is also a happy one — compact, not showy, and perfectly balanced. As for the colour scheme, it would be a crime not to describe its wayward variations in the minutest detail. The chancel walls are green, the roof blue with a white cornice. The chancel arch is of exposed yellow brick but its capitals are picked out in turquoise. Lilac is the colour favoured for the walls of the nave, white for its roof. But the visible tie-beams are painted orange and the cornice is turquoise once more. The furnishings are a light yellow-brown, the nave floor of yellow bricks, the chancel floor of stone flags. A cornice of miniature pendant Gothick arches runs around the otherwise plain, canted chancel roof. The nave roof is also canted and ceiled but has the tie-beams exposed. The chancel arch is chamfered and has moulded capitals. All this is probably of 1767 and eminently worthy of inspection.

Font: C15; octagonal; bowl with various leaf designs and two shields.
Housel bench: C17; tapering legs with a top rosette; band of guilloche.
Box pews: c1767, as are all the following; plain panelling.
Chancel panelling: Continuous pierced leaf cresting; centre with plain pointed arches.
Chancel rail: Tall, slender turned balusters; panelled newels.
Communion rail: Ditto.
Communion table: Solid; plain Tuscan pilasters at angles.
Font cover: Octagonal base; ogee canopy.
Musicians' pew: Raised higher at the west end; plain panelling.
Pulpit: A three-decker; plain panelling; top frieze of crenellation; the reader's and clerk's desks integral with the box pews.
Royal Arms: Carved; tiny; of George III.
Organ: Early C19; tripartite front; raised centre with a crocketed ogee arch; straight side sections with crenellations and pinnacles.

123

Petersham

South transept

Petersham church enjoys a semi-rural setting of a kind denied to most churches in or close to London. Its backcloth is the sweep of Richmond Hill with the grassy slopes and the wood above. At the foot, for contrast, Georgian and neo-Georgian red brick groups itself around the bends in the road. It is at this point that the church will be found. Of extreme picturesqueness, the building lies hidden a few yards up an alleyway, invisible from the road, and the impression is one of brick walls and small trees framing a jumbled exterior. The churchyard is narrow and crowded here, like a second alleyway, but is much more spacious round to the east. The setting is of an intimacy fully appropriate to a church whose informal accretions over the centuries cannot be, with the notable exceptions of Minstead and Whitby, outmatched anywhere.

It is quite a task at first sight, to disentangle the various parts, let alone the correct orientation. A stroll around to the opposite side will, however, make things easier. One must bear in mind that the tower is a west tower and that the long section parallel to the alleyway is, in fact, the south transept. The building is medieval in origin, though little of that is visible inside or out. The chancel belongs to the second half of the thirteenth century, but of this only a blocked lancet on the north side tells. Even the buttresses here cannot be trusted, and the walls, in any case, are rendered now. Whatever nave went with this chancel was swept away during the post-Reformation era. The west tower seems to be of the seventeenth century and as a drawing of about 1800 shows, originally projected as usual.

Now it is partly enclosed by the wide south transept. The tower is of brick, like the rest of the post-medieval church, and has two stages divided by a low-profile string-course, a plain, pointed west window, and an embattled parapet. The pointed bell-openings contain unusual and quite pretty brick tracery of horizontal and vertical bands. There is also a lovely octagonal wooden cupola with plain arched openings and an ogee lead dome carrying a ball finial.

Much was done to enlarge the church during the eighteenth century, possibly in 1790, the date of the porch and vestry. The latter is attached to the north side of the tower and has a simple wooden window of domestic provenance. The porch stands in front of the tower. Its doorway has a segmental arch with keystone and abaci. The north transept was added, or perhaps rebuilt from an earlier one, at this time, too. There is a large, round-arched window in the east wall, with a circular window above to light the gallery. An attempt was made to give the north wall a proper facade. There are three windows here, a lunette in the centre, and two with segmental arches low down under the gallery. These are repeated just around the corners in the east and west walls. The wall is crowned by a broken pediment-cum-gable, with brick dentils, containing a circular window. New windows were inserted in the east and south walls of the chancel; they are segment-headed, and that to the east contains inset wooden Y-tracery. The long south transept is of 1840, built to replace a pre-existing, late seventeenth or eighteenth-century one. It has three round-arched windows in all three sides set in deep, rendered reveals. There is also a

Children's seats

circular window at the north end on the east side. The transept has a brick corbel table or, if one speaks with a classicist's voice, a dentil frieze. The brickwork is of a richer variety than that of the north transept, etc. Also of 1840 is the staircase projection south of the porch. It gives access to the galleries and has a lean-to roof with a brick cornice.

The first impression gained upon entering is one of spacial confusion. The inclination is to look left and right, the eye following the rhythms of the pews and galleries, the wide, flat ceiling running straight across, and the spaciousness of these areas. It is only after a realization that an altar is absent in the place where one expects it to occur that the building's true orientation becomes clear. For the chancel, with its deeper, mellowed glow lies straight ahead, and as one enters one stands in what was originally a normal nave. The nave has been completely negated spacially, its walls taken out, its shape absorbed into the transepts. There is nothing medieval left. The walls are painted a salmon pink, the ceilings white. The chancel is framed by a shallow segmental arch, almost Soanian in its precision. Set into this is an entablature on plain pilasters and the area above is solid. This feature, the only architectural one inside, must be late eighteenth century. Two points concerning the furnishings need making before this account is closed. Firstly, the benches in the south transept have little tip-up seats for children, a rare occurrence. Secondly, the chandeliers are recent replacements of run-of-the-mill electric bulbs. How very much more appropriate they are, so superior to the insensitive lighting of too many churches. But then Petersham is cared for by a group of Friends.

Communion rail: C17; vertically-symmetrical turned balusters.

North gallery: C18; on thin iron columns; plain fronts.

Pulpit: 1796; high up on an Ionic column; panelling with lattice work; leaf frieze; back-post with a broken pediment; winding stairs with wrought-iron rail with vertical drop shapes and scrolls.

Reader's desk: 1796(?); plain panelling; back-post with broken pediment; reeded book-rest.

Font: 1797; a stone baluster; by John Long.

Font cover: 1797; octagonal; ribbed ogee dome with finial.

Panelling: Early C19; behind the altar; with depressed arches.

Royal Arms: 1810; carved; of George III.

Benches: c1840; open backs; tip-up side seats; painted red.

Box pews: c1840 (some may be C18); plain panelling; rounded corners to two blocks; numbered; also red.

South & west galleries: c1840; as north gallery.

Also one hatchment and three chandeliers of traditional type. The Victorian communion table is mercifully concealed from view.

Warminghurst

Exterior from the south-west

Interior looking east

Warminghurst should be approached from the south; as one travels along the narrow, winding lane, deep-sunk between banks and hedges, the church suddenly appears with a bang through the tunnel of foliage. There it stands, tall and proud, on its knoll, surrounded by the peace and beauty of this hilly Weald country. Only a farm accompanies it. An old brick wall, sweeping round in an elegant curve, encloses the churchyard, which offers a splendid view south to Chanctonbury Ring. The church literally oozes unrestored character, the rough stone walls being devoid of any interference. The shapes, too, are noble and highly satisfying, clearly defined and of perfect proportions. A surprising variety of materials occurs; stone, brick, tile-hanging, shingles. Yet they blend so harmoniously together, an object lesson for all modern architects who, striving consciously to achieve the same ends, overstep the mark time and time again. The old lamp by the gate is just right.

The church has a nave and chancel in one, with a bell-turret above the west gable, a south porch, and a north vestry. Nave and chancel are thirteenth century, of that artless yet moving Early English which one often finds in Sussex (eg, Up Marden). The west window, set high up, is a plain circle. It is not even given a proper chamfer. Nor are the four lancet windows along the south wall. The east window is a replacement of about 1300. It has three trefoiled lights and three unencircled quarterfoils in bar tracery above. The chancel has angle buttresses of one set-off. The west doorway is Perpendicular and has a depressed arch under a straight hood-mould. What is the date of the bell-turret? It is probably medieval in essence though it has, of course, been re-covered on many occasions. Like so many in the south-east of England, it is really dateless now. Never mind for, with its tile-hung sides and shingled spire, it must be considered one of the loveliest in Sussex. This type of spire, with the cardinal faces splayed at the foot and the diagonal faces tapering to a point, has recently been christened the splayed-foot type. It occurs often in the south-east (eg, Brenzett, Kent). A vestry was added on the north side of the church during the late sixteenth or early seventeenth century. Its north window is of three segmentally-arched lights with continuous rolls under a straight hood-mould, a typical Gothic Survival piece. The doorway is a pastiche of the fifteenth-century west doorway, except that it has the same rolls as the window. The brick south porch, featureless now, is eighteenth century. It is rapidly disappearing beneath an outgrowth of vegetation. The north windows of nave and chancel are eighteenth-century brick reconstructions of thirteenth century lancets.

The interior is perfect, free of pomp and ceremony, cool yet endearing. Light floods in through the east window, bathing the sanctuary, silhouetting the arches of the screen and bringing to life the panelling of the pews. It throws into sharp relief the surfaces of the stone floor, worn and pockmarked as they are by the passing feet of generations of worshippers. In the chancel, small black diamond shapes are set into the corners of the slabs. The chancel roof is ceiled but that of the nave has its rafters exposed. It is single-framed, with collars on arched braces and only a couple of tie-beams. Like all such roofs, it produces exciting effects of light and shade. The date is probably thirteenth century. The thirteenth-century south doorway can now be approached only from inside the nave. It has a continuous roll moulding. The vestry doorway, of about 1600, is identical to that outside. The crowning achievement of the interior is, of course, the stately screen and tympanum, the latter introducing a splash of colour into a scheme of browns and creams and green foliage seen through clear glass.

Pulpit stairs

Such tympana are rare, and to come across one so beautifully preserved is singularly pleasing. The arches of the screen define the view of the sanctuary, indeed intensify the emotional content of that modest table and cross. Warminghurst was restored, or rather conserved, in 1959. The firm involved, Denman & Son, fully deserves recording.

Communion rail: c1707-14(?); with slender twisted balusters.
Communion table: c1707-14(?); with twisted legs.
Screen: c1707-14; three keystoned arches, with a thin roll, on square panelled posts; plain panelling above.
Tympanum: c1707-14; with the Royal Arms of Queen Anne; background of red drapery on a blue field.
Font: C18; a stone baluster; octagonal bowl.
Font cover bracket: C18; attached to wall above; wrought-iron; many scrolls; the cover has disappeared.
Box pews: Late C18; panels with blank trefoiled arches.
Pulpit: Late C18; a three-decker; plain panelling; stairs with turned balusters; reader's and clerk's desks part of pews; book-rest on good brackets reminiscent of the sharply curved bill of an eagle.
Also three hatchments.

Brougham (Ninekirk)

To those who like their churches to be hidden in secret places far from the indifferent glance of the casual passer-by, Ninekirk must forever remain the exemplar. For surely no other church is so remotely situated as this — not remote in the sense of uninhabited countryside, but in being placed away from all roads and reached only by an overgrown bridleway. The track wends an undulating course, keeping parallel to the River Eden, first through a cornfield, then down into a wild hollow, up again across more fields, and finally dropping through more wildness to a meadow. The church, in its deep seclusion, stands ready to welcome those who have made this pilgrimage through the Westmorland landscape. It lies long and low in a broad churchyard surrounded by a stone wall, facing across the Eden. The backcloth, with the craggy red sandstone cliffs glimpsed through a screen of trees, would have satisfied even that paragon of the Picturesque, Richard Payne Knight. The east view is closed by the distant Pennines.

Ninekirk was rebuilt in 1660 by Lady Anne Clifford, Countess of Pembroke. She was a very remarkable woman. In 1649, at the age of seventy, she settled on her estates in the north. Instead of making one house comfortable for her declining years, she rebuilt them all, and also three churches. Her properties included Appleby Castle, Brougham Castle and Brough Castle in Westmorland, Barden Tower and Skipton Castle in the West Riding. The churches are Ninekirk and St Wilfred, Brougham, and Mallerstang. Concerning Ninekirk she wrote: 'It would in all likelyhood have fallen down it was soe ruiness if it had not bin repaired by me'.

The church consists of a continuous nave and chancel, with that ground-hugging profile characteristic of the north. Only the bellcote breaks this horizontality. Red sandstone is the material of the walls, and slates grey with lichens cover the roof. The motifs are pure Gothic Survival and, if it were not for the east and west facades, could easily be mistaken for a genuine late Perpendicular building of the time of Henry VIII. The bellcote has a gable and a single plain opening. All windows are single, uncusped, round-arched lights under straight hood-moulds. To east and west a pair of such windows occur, separated by middle buttresses. There are buttresses along each side, too, and they all have one set-off. The priest's doorway has a segmental arch under a straight hood-mould, the south doorway a round arch with a continuous chamfer. All this is almost identical to St Wilfred's (of 1658), even down to the disposition of the windows. The porch is an addition of 1841; it does no harm.

Inside, the visitor will be transported straight back to the time of Lady Clifford. Indeed, if she could enter her church today she would feel immediately at home. Nothing has changed since the seventeenth century. No other 'prayer-

Exterior from the south

Interior looking east

book' interior captures quite so felicitously the sense of time suspended in reverence of a single patron's munificent love of architecture. It is as self-contained, and even perhaps a little disquieting, as those carefully preserved homes of certain writers such as Kipling and Wordsworth. Above the reredos, and enclosed in a laurel wreath, appears the initials AP for Anne Pembroke, and the date 1660. Only the communion rail is a little later, being an addition of about 1685. A note in the parish register of that year states: 'We have all things in good order in and about our church except our altar which wants a rayling and that wee intend to get done quickly'. The furnishings are so clearly segregated that they appear as if arrayed for a tour of inspection, and so neat and beguiling that they might be standing in a furniture designer's showroom. Apart from the gilding on the reredos, bright colours are absent; instead there occur greyish stone floors, brown woodwork and white walls. The crisp-looking roof has collars on spreading arched braces; there are also longitudinal braces. Ninekerk is as single-minded, and as much the product of one person's individualism, as the more magnificent Staunton Harold.

Chest: Medieval; plain. The following furnishings are all of c1660-3; individual dates are given where known.
Almsbox: 1663; a small box on a wooden pillar.
Box pews: 1661; plain panelling.
Communion table: With turned legs.
Family pews: Identical, but the west are larger; panelling as box pews; canopies with tall turned balusters; panelled tops; metal hat pegs.
Font: 1662; stone; octagonal; plain.
Pulpit (with tester): A two-decker; plain panelling; book-rest on large, flat, wavy brackets; plainly panelled back-post; tester with crenellations and moulded pendants.
Reredos: Raised semi-circular lunette above centre; plain panels with Ten Commandments, Lord's Prayer and Creed.
Screen: Tall turned balusters; inset flat, pierced, ogee-trefoiled arches.
Vestry: As screen; is this original?
Communion rail: c1685; with turned dumb-bell balusters.
Also three hatchments.

Inglesham

Inglesham is a church which can easily be missed by the casual tourist, standing as it does among farm buildings some hundred yards off the main Highworth-Lechlade road. That is a pity, for this church preserves an interior practically unique in the country. Others, such as Gayhurst or Shobdon, which date from one stylistic moment, may present a more unified picture, but from the point of view of studied informality and historical continuity, Inglesham cannot be matched by any other English church.

It is approached along a narrow, winding track and has a Georgian house upon its right, an older farm to its left and, directly opposite, the severe lines of a modern Dutch barn. The church, too, is severe in its outline, openly rectangular with its aggregate of cubes and its plain, straight parapets. This austerity is relieved by the tracery forms of the windows and bellcote, and by the pair of gargoyles which stare menacingly down towards the visitor. The building material is stone, used both for the walls and the roofing slates, its surface partly concealed by patches of old rendering and a generous coating of lichens.

The plan consists of a nave, with a bellcote above the west gable, north and south aisles, chancel, south chapel, and a south porch, quite a complex arrangement for so small a church. Yet this, with the one exception of the porch, is the original layout and dates from about 1200. The bellcote, with its plate tracery, is an addition of about 1270, however. A window of similar character and date can be seen in the chancel south wall, and the north doorway, with its rounded-trefoiled arch, belongs to the first half of the thirteenth century. The steep roof of the porch suggests that this, too, was built during the Early English period. About 1290 a new, larger window was inserted in the chancel east wall. It is of three stepped, pointed-trefoiled lights under a single arch, a form that occurs quite often in the Upper Thames region. Certain alterations were carried out during the fifteenth century, viz, the rebuilding of the aisles with new windows and plain parapets, a new nave west window, and changes in the porch. Finally, the south chapel received a new east window in the seventeenth century.

Upon entering, the first impression is one of total confusion. Vistas are everywhere broken up by screens, and the architectural features emerge waist-deep from among the box pews. After the visitor has taken his bearings, it is advised that he examine the architecture first, although in the overall scheme of things this is of secondary importance. The arcades belong to the original building of about 1200 and enclose a short, yet high nave of almost Anglo-Saxon proportions. The double-chamfered arches are round on the south, pointed on the north, indicating that the south arcade came first. Capitals are of two forms; early stiff-leaf or decorated trumpet-scallops. The abaci are octagonal and the piers circular. Against the north wall of the chancel is a length of black arcading, round-arched with filleted rolls and more stiff-leaf capitals. This runs for only half the chancel's length, proving that the work of about 1290 included an extension eastwards. The chancel arch, incidentally, is a companion to the north arcade. All these

Exterior from the south-west

View across west end

features are the product of a local workshop undertaking commissions during the final decade of the twelfth century. Other examples of its work, which forms a textbook of Transitional design, exist at Faringdon in Berkshire and Kelmscott, Langford and Little Faringdon in Oxfordshire.

The character of the interior, however, is determined not by these admittedly excellent features, but by the incredible *pot-pourri* of woodwork. Box pews fill the nave and west bays of the aisles and spill over into the chancel. The east bay of each aisle is partitioned by medieval screens, all in an incredibly unrestored condition. There is also a pulpit with tester piling up in one corner. The walls also deserve attention. They display a wonderful patchwork of creams, browns, greys and pinks, overlaid in many places by fragmentary remains of texts. Then there are those small human touches which, although having nothing to do with the history of art, add immeasurable charm wherever they occur. Such is the plan of the church hanging from a truly venerable iron lamp bracket, impossible to date. Above all, however, is the feeling of continuity engendered by so many features of so wide a time span, from the late Saxon sculpture in the south aisle to the royal arms of

William IV over the north doorway. Yet even more remarkable is the visual unity of it all, every item contributing to the whole and blending happily with its neighbour. And it remains as relevant and immediate to us today as it did to our ancestors of two and three hundred years ago.

Relief sculpture: Early C11; in the south aisle wall; the Virgin and Child with the Hand of God.
Reredos: c1330; a few fragmentary pinnacles and patches of colour.
Font: C15; octagonal; plain stem; bowl with quarterfoils enclosing roses.
Screens: C15; three; one-light divisions with tracery in the head of each light; bands of leaf above and below.
Pulpit (with tester): Late C16; plain panelling.
Font cover: Early C17; octagonal; pyramidal; plain.
Squire's and Vicar's pews: Early C17; in the chancel; plain panelling, decorated lunette shapes along top.
Box pews: C18; plain panelling.
Box pews: Early C19; in the north-west corner; ditto.
Royal Arms: c1830-7; of William IV.

Box pews: detail

Mildenhall

Mildenhall is a Kennet Valley village set between gentle downland east of Marlborough. The church lies south of the village centre, down a lane, but is not isolated since it is the centrepiece of a secondary group of houses and cottages. It is a leafy, semi-rural setting, the churchyard partly mown, partly left wild. To the east, open views along the valley prevail. The walls of the church are a wonderful textured patchwork of

Exterior from the west

flint and stone, also with much later repair work in brick (south aisle, tower, etc). The chancel has a stone-slated roof, the others being of lead. The elevations are not particularly elegant, but they are charecterful nonetheless and suggest a church preserving something of more than common interest.

That interest begins outside with the ground stage of the triple-staged west tower. The ground stage is Anglo-Saxon and possibly of about 804, the year in which the Bishop of Winchester acquired land at Mildenhall for a new church. The window, now blocked, consists of a tiny, triangular-headed light surrounded by heavy stone blocks. It is an odd looking affair, and may have suffered alteration at some point. The middle stage is Norman, as can be seen by the former two-light bell openings to north and south. They have the typical dividing shaft. This tower extension marks the beginning of a rebuilding campaign that starts about 1150 and ends with the north aisle about 1200. But, apart from the tower, and also the priest's doorway, nothing of all this shows externally. The doorway has a plain, round arch. Next to it is a thirteenth-century lancet with a head at the apex of the hood-mould. The south aisle west window is also thirteenth century but may have been altered about 1815. Of the thirteenth century, too, is the tower west doorway; it has a continuous roll. Above is a window which looks superficially Norman but may well be a Saxon window re-cut.

The fifteenth to sixteenth century did much. The tower was heightened, the nave given a clerestory, and new windows inserted everywhere. So the exterior now looks Perpendicular. The two-light bell-openings proudly display that most lovely of tracery forms known as Somerset tracery, ie, patterns cut into solid stonework. The parapet is embattled. The clerestory windows are straight-headed but have simple panel tracery. Other windows have, variously, two and four-centred arches. The east windows are three-lighters, that in the chancel quite tall. Of 1815-6 is the most interesting feature, perhaps, of the exterior, the central clerestory window on the south side. It is a plain arched light containing glazing bars in the form of geometrical tracery in the style of Westminster Abbey. It is a prelude to the Gothick pleasures inside. The south porch, no doubt, is also early nineteenth century, with its thin details, as is the plain, battered buttress alongside.

The interior was completely refurnished in 1815-6, as the following inscription in the chancel confirms: '1816 This Church deeply in decay has been all but rebuilded generously and piously at their own expense', they being the churchwardens and other patrons. The furnishings are entirely in the Gothick style and are wonderfully complete, rich and bold, although a little heavy-going. Yet they are immeasurably fresher than the ponderous woodwork of the Victorian age. The furnishings fill the interior completely, but they are so carefully designed that a feeling of overcrowding does not occur. There is a truly lovely gallery, its front recessed in an elegant concavity, repeated below in the pews as they stand back in deference to the font. Even the south doorway is given a Gothick surround with crenellation, friezes and thin, reeded shafting. The nave roof was also provided with a new wooden cornice. The decorative motifs applied to the furnishings are still very much pre-archaeological; see, for example, the little pierced and embattled gables on the testers or the broad ogees which occur everywhere. They provide just the right amount of lightheartedness needed to bring the furnishings to life. A rare occurrence is the arrangement of twin pulpit and reader's

desk placed either side of the chancel arch. For comparisons one must go to Easton in Dorset or Leighton Bromswold in Huntingdonshire.

The architecture is inevitably an appendix to the furnishings. The tower arch, concealed by panelling, comes first. Its twelfth-century responds remain and have pendant lobes. After that comes the three-bay south arcade with round, single-stepped arches, square abaci, circular piers and trumpet-scallop capitals, some with leaf enrichment, one with heads. It is a typically Transitional *ensemble*, as is the chancel arch, pointed this time, and double-chamfered. The inner chamfer rests upon corbels with more trumpet scallops, a head (north) and waterleaf (south). The north arcade brings us up to about 1200. It has the same single-stepped round arches and circular piers, but also circular abaci and moulded capitals. The roofs are early seventeenth century. That of the chancel is a plastered barrel vault with exposed rib panelling. At the intersections occur pretty leaf bosses. The nave roof has tie-beams, lozenge-shaped kingposts, the same bosses, and strange leaf pendants.

All furnishings are of 1815-6

Box pews: Gothick panelling with ogee arches, buttress-shafts with leaf terminations, lozenges and triangles carrying tripartite leaf motifs; blocks raised against side walls; blocks set back concavely around font.

Chancel panelling: Continuous leaf cresting; richly cusped panelling; much leaf decoration.

Choir stalls: Like the box pews with ogee panelling, leaf bands and lozenges.

Communion rails: Balusters carrying trefoiled arches; lozenge bands; the red leather kneelers date from 1796.

Font: Octagonal; bowl with quarterfoils and leaf on underside; thin panelled stem.

Font cover: Hexagonal; pyramidal; leaf finial with a tall *fleche;* applied ogees.

Pulpit (with tester): Ogee-headed panelling with Symbols of the Passion in vesicae; stairs with turned balusters; tall panelled backpost with a vesica; square-tester with convex centre and a pierced cresting with embattled gables, arches and spiky pinnacles.

Reader's desk: Ditto.

Reredos: Raised semi-circular centre with pierced, crocketed ogee cresting; tall pinnacles on tall, thin shafts with leaf capitals; Ten Commandments in centre; outer panels with leaf cresting containing Lord's Prayer and Creed.

Royal Arms: Of George III; frame with extruded corners enclosing paterae.

Tower screens: Solid panelling filling the arch; panels with arched heads.

West gallery: Concave front with ogee-headed panels divided by reed-like shafting; inner trefoil- headed panels, some with Benefactions.

Also three hatchments.

Interior looking east

The Gothick clerestory window

Old Dilton

Exterior from the west

The first view of Old Dilton, if approached from the west, is of the church suddenly and dramatically framed in a railway arch. The east prospect is quieter but still unexpected. It is a peaceful, rural setting, despite the nearness to Westbury and the occasional passage of a train high up on the embankment. The latter cuts off the churchyard and sports a stand of trees which rises high above the church. Perhaps the embankment has helped to make the churchyard more lush than it might otherwise have been, containing the moisture and encouraging luxuriant growth. For lush it certainly is, a haven of natural beauty and a paradise for wild flowers. At the time of our visit at least ten species were in bloom including red campion, lady's smock, and most appropriate of all, common star of Bethlehem. Redundancy can sometimes be beneficial! The east side is bordered by a stream which trickles half-hidden through a deep canyon of overhanging banks. The music of the water mingles and forms a duet with the clucking of hens in a nearby garden.

The church is very individualistic, perhaps even idiosyncratic, with its broad and low elevations and the bellcote perched above the west gable supported by its own buttress. The bellcote is ashlar-faced but the walls are of random stonework; the roofs are of stone slates. The plan consists of a nave with a south porch, a chancel, and a long north aisle with an east vestry. All this appears to be late medieval, ie, Perpendicular, nothing being earlier than the fourteenth century. It seems that the whole church was rebuilt at this time, as it is unlikely that at least one older feature would not have survived a gradual programme of replacement. But that does not explain the occurrence of features which can be dated from the fourteenth century to the early sixteenth century. The porch is fourteenth century and has an entrance with continuous mouldings and trefoiled spandrels. Also fourteenth century is the south doorway with its segmental arch. The two windows in the south side of the chancel are fourteenth century, too. They are of two and three cusped, ogee-headed lights under a straight hood-mould. A north aisle was added in the fifteenth century. Its windows are again straight-headed but the individual lights are round-arched and cusped. Is the blocked doorway here fifteenth century? The arch is a strange, flat trefoiled affair. The south-east nave window is also fifteenth century and identical to those in the aisle except that, this time, the lights are pointed.

Of the early sixteenth century we have the bellcote, the nave south-west and twin west windows, and the priest's doorway. The bellcote is of a type found on other Wiltshire churches (eg, Great Chalfield) and has an octagonal lower stage partly projecting and supported by a central buttress. Each face has two tiers of tiny, paired bell openings, really just basic sound holes, and the whole is crowned by a pyramidal spire. The ball finial suggests repairs in the seventeenth or eighteenth century. The twin west windows below are of two plain, arched lights, straight-headed, and without hood-moulds. The westernmost window in the south wall of the nave is identical. The priest's doorway has a depressed arch. Now the seventeenth century contributions. A vestry was built against the north side of the chancel; its north wall cuts into the north-east buttress of the aisle. A new window was inserted in the nave south wall and is distinguishable by its plain, square-headed lights under a straight head. Finally, the chancel east window. This, with its three stepped lights under one arch looks suspiciously eighteenth century. Altogether, the exterior of Old Dilton presents quite a textbook of late medieval, etc, window variations.

One enters the church now through the priest's doorway and is at once confronted by an interior crowded with 'prayer-book' furnishings, perfect in its unalloyed authenticity. Yet one's enjoyment is saddened by the knowledge that Old Dilton is redundant now; rarely do an incumbent's feet tread the stairs up to the pulpit, and only infrequently does the sanctuary receive the reaffirmation of the communicants. The interior is inevitably, under such circumstances, something of a museum piece. Such thoughts, of course, are engengered by other redundant churches but seem to flow more readily here. Still, the Redundant Churches Fund has done its usual exemplary job of conservation. Furnishings crowd into every nook and cranny. There are ample box pews, taller in the aisle, a three-decker in the customary position half-way down one side, two galleries, and even a clock, the latter a lovely piece. Only the chancel space is left free. The walls are newly whitewashed, the floors yellow-grey flagstones, the furnishings a light brown. The fifteenth-century three-bay north arcade has panelled arches, as they occur at Corsham and in other Wiltshire churches. The piers are octagonal, the capitals shapeless and obviously interfered with. The nave is ceiled barrel-wise but has the tie-beams exposed, and even they are plastered. The chancel roof is flat. I have seen it stated that the Fund has not as yet been called upon to preserve *historic* churches. Yet by what other term could one describe Old Dilton with its unrestored texture and period interior?

Benches: C15; plain, panelled, straight-topped ends.
Font: C15; octagonal; bowl with quarterfoils; stem with cusped panels.
Communion table: C17; turned legs; top frieze of strapwork-like vine trailing.
Benefaction board: C18, as are all the following; plain frame.
Box pews: Plain panelling; some incorporate re-used medieval bench ends; raised up at west end of north aisle.
Clock: Octagonal face; beautiful numerals; fleur-de-lis; on a tall, panelled stem; by Cook of Warminster.
Communion rail: Plain, square balusters; the rail rises concavely each end.
Family pews: As box pews but taller.
North & west galleries: Plain panelling.
Painted text: The Lord's Prayer.
Pulpit (with tester): A three-decker; all parts with plain panelling; curving up stairs with square balusters; plainly panelled back-post; thin tester with modillion cornice; clerk's desk with convex front.
Royal Arms: Of George III.

Interior from the gallery

The clock

Robin Hood's Bay

Exterior from the west

Robin Hood's Bay is one of the show villages of England. Its picturesqueness is justifiably famous. The houses, of diverse materials but mainly with red pantile roofs, tumble down the steep slopes to the wide sweep of the cliff-sheltered bay. Narrow streets, twisting passages, and a variety of levels characterise its irresistable charms. The church, for better or for worse, takes no part in all this, being situated almost a mile outside the village on the edge of the moors. The setting is windswept and lonely, with a panoramic view down the valley to the distant sea. The church and its environs possess a rugged picturesqueness of their own, but visitors are normally so intent on enjoying the village that few bother to stop. The building's more subtle allure seems to elude the casual tourist. Perhaps it is because the external appearance resembles some nameless chapel in any industrial town. Yet that is only superficially true, as we shall see.

The exterior is certainly dour, perhaps even a little cold, with its precise, dark, grey-brown ashlar walls and its sparse enrichment. The difference in scale between nave and chancel is surprising; the latter looks as if it were an afterthought, which, of course, it is not. The church was built in 1821 and has not been altered since except for the addition of two mighty fortress-like buttresses at the east end. They are extremely impressive. The octagonal wooden cupola has a weatherboarded base, open arcading with raised, semi-circular heads *a la* text boards, and an ogee dome of lead carrying a ball finial. The porch has a round-arched entrance below a pedimental gable. The windows are all plain, pointed lights with lovely intersecting glazing bars. Their hood-moulds are thin and flat and rest upon equally flat, bracket-like label stops. On the north side the windows are cut short to allow for the gallery. Before going inside, do not overlook the unusual herringbone tooling of the stonework or the clusters of wavy-topped headstones.

The interior is amazingly complete; one should be grateful, after all, that the Victorians built a new church down in the village, thus saving ours from a fate worse than death. Nothing is earlier than 1821 and nothing has been changed since. It is as complete a statement for its date as are Leweston and Ninekirk for theirs. Here occur a perfect suite of box pews painted pink and coffee, a towering three-decker pulpit, galleries painted grey and white, the north with a separate section for the leading family distinguished by its stained panelling, and a delightfully rustic little font cover. The stone floor is of a beautiful brown colour. The crowning touch is the seaweed hung up in the chancel. The segmental chancel arch is absolutely plain, as are the flat; ceiled roofs. Although services are held here only occasionally, the church is not in the least neglected. Indeed, a small museum connected with maritime activities is maintained inside. There is a model in a case and also implements, etc. So interest in the building is being sustained, as the fresh flowers on the altar show. Let us hope that the long-term future of this important church remains secure and that the dark shadow of redundancy will not be cast over it.

All the furnishings are of c1821.

Benefaction boards: Gothick; with ogee-arched heads.

Box pews: Plain panelling; raised theatrically at the west end; numbered.

Commandment boards: With the usual raised, semi-circular tops.

Communion rail: With plain, square balusters.

Family pew: Incorporated in the north gallery; panelling with inturned corners separated by fluted pilasters.

Font: An urn-shaped stone baluster.

Font cover: Octagonal; flat; plain newel supporting eight rough, turned balusters set pyramid-wise.

North & west galleries: On Tuscan columns; plain panelling; large staircase dividing into two; plain balusters.

Pulpit (with tester): A tall three-decker; all parts with plain panelling curving up to each section; curving up stairs with slim, turned balusters; separate plain tester.

Royal Arms: 1822; of George IV; the frame has raised segmental top.

Squire's & Vicar's pews: Set around the chancel arch; as box pews but taller.

Also one hatchment.

East end from the gallery

In the north gallery

Skelton (Old Church)

Chancel east window

Skelton old church lies concealed in a wooded enclave north of the main road, immediately where the latter, via a double bend, sweeps into the village. A drive leads off into the trees, and as one ascends the causewayed footpath to the churchyard gate, the eye is greeted by a sight of serene beauty. The church adopts a supportive role at the rear of a churchyard that is rapidly turning back to nature, not in the sense of bramble and nettle-strewn undergrowth, but in the sense of a slowly evolving wood. So there are saplings pushing up through the grass, a white covering of hedge parsley, meadow cranesbill everywhere, and older, taller trees encompassing this veritable reserve. It is a haven for birds and other animals free of pesticides, insecticides, chemical fertilizers, and all the other life-destroying adjuncts of the twentieth century.

The church, to repeat, seems a castaway amongst all this greenery. Yet it possesses attractions of its own which complement those of the churchyard. The plan consists of a west tower, a nave with attached north chapel, and a chancel. All this, with the exception of the apparently medieval chancel, dates from 1785. The ashlar walling is tooled in exactly the same herringbone pattern as at Robin Hood's Bay and, although the latter is Skelton's junior by thirty-five years, must have been built by the same family of masons. The roofs are of blue slates. The west tower is a very undemonstrative affair, superficially Gothick, with its pointed west window containing intersecting glazing bars, and its embattled parapet. Perhaps castellated would be a more historically appropriate term for the latter feature. The bell-openings are round-arched instead. The tower is narrower than the nave and allows for two tiers of square windows here, the upper for

the gallery. The nave side windows are round-arched, too, and have intersecting glazing bars as in the tower. The chancel south window is the same but has ordinary glazing bars. So has the east window of Venetian type with its heavy, plain, somewhat Vanbrughian frames. There is also a plain, round-arched priest's doorway.

The interior is one of the saddest spectacles in the whole of England. Here is a perfect 'prayer-book' interior rapidly deteriorating. Filfth, dust and rubbish cover the floor, plaster is falling from the walls, floors are collapsing, box pews are coming apart, the gallery is in a dangerous condition. At every breath of wind the whole east window creaks and groans; an east gale could well send it crashing down across the communion rail. There are warning notices everywhere. Behind a pew lay a dead squirrel stuck to the floor, the bitter culmination of a century's neglect. The communion table has disappeared; defeat emanates from every rotting floorboard, from every battered panel, from every gaping hole in the plaster. It is a spiritually debilitating experience and one longs to return to the living beauty of the churchyard.

Why is the church in such a condition? The answer is even more unbelievable than the crazy situation at Pilling. About a hundred years ago a feud over pew rights developed between the parishioners and the squire. In the end the parishioners withdrew, built their own church in 1884, and left the old one to rot. But that is only half the story for, even today, the village will have nothing to do with the old church! It seems incredible that insularity and bigotry of this kind concerning something which took place so long ago can exist in an English village today. What is more to the point, however, is that this

Interior looking west

Chancel interior

insularity is causing one particular part of our heritage to disintegrate. What can be done? The present incumbent is sympathetic towards rehabilitation but needs to tread warily. He quite rightly does not wish to see the church converted for other purposes. The only answer is to declare the building redundant and transfer it to the Fund. Otherwise its fate will be that of Goltho in Lincolnshire or Shireshead in Lancashire. Is that what Skelton wants? Surely it is as worth saving for future generations as Old Dilton, or Parracombe, or Little Washbourne. But time is running out.

All furnishings are of c1785.

Box pews: Plain panelling; numbered; names of pew-renters along the walls.

Commandment boards: With segmental tops.

Communion rail: With turned balusters.

Family pews: Really the north chapel; plain panelled front.

Pulpit (with tester): A sweet three-decker; pulpit with plain panelling and chamfered corners; back-post with demi-shafts set into the angles; pretty tester with chamfered corners, a running trail, dentils and a cresting of waves; reader's desk book-rest on wavy brackets.

West gallery: On four fluted posts; front with plain panelling; steep tiers of seating.

Also a royal arms.

Whitby

Whitby is the unrestored church *par excellence*. Not even Minstead, not even Petersham can rival its incredible accretions or match its interior of gallery after gallery, of pews and family pews crowded together. The church lies, low and spreading, up on the windy east cliff, overlooking the grey North Sea and the busy harbour of this delightful little fishing town. It has for company the noble ruins of the great and venerable abbey, where that decisive synod of 664 took place. What a contrast there is between the church and the abbey, the former with its even, castellated elevations, the latter with gables, pinnacles and fragments of sky enclosed within empty arches. Below is the further contrast of the cliff with its hummocks of grass interspersed among the rocks, and the gulls drifting effortlessly by. The churchyard is open, bare in its treeless expanse, and particularised by a good crop of wavy-topped headstones.

The architectural history is complex and must be fully elucidated. All parts are characterised by a certain squatness of elevation, as if the church has been scythed by the gales. The walls are rough and weathered, more so on the medieval south side. The story begins in the first half of the twelfth century when a church of nave and chancel was erected. This was as

long as the present building, quite exceptional for a Norman parish church. As medieval churches were built from east to west, we will take the chancel first. It still has its corbel table, its pilaster buttresses, and a group of three stepped windows in the east wall. There survive also two windows in the north wall and one in the south. All these windows were blocked up in 1650 and reopend only in 1910. The battlements are later, possibly thirteenth or fourteenth century. The chancel thus still keeps its Norman character. So does the whole nave south wall which, in spite of the later windows, displays a severe ruggedness which could belong to no other century. There is, first of all, the south doorway placed mid-way, a curious instance of symmetry. It has a two-stepped arch and two orders of shafts carrying spiral volute capitals. Above the present porch occurs a blocked window further east which has subsequently been lengthened into the form of an amazingly attenuated lancet. The buttressing is as in the chancel.

Next in order of time comes the west tower, an addition of about 1190. It is a bleak, stubby structure with heavy, nook-shafted clasping buttresses, extra buttresses to the west, a round-arched west window, and pointed bell-openings flanked by blank arcading. The battlements are as elsewhere. The whole west side was altered in the eighteenth century. During the first half of the thirteenth century long transepts were added. The north was remodelled later but the south preserves its shape intact. Of details there are only the fragment of a lancet window in the north transept east wall, the finely-moulded surround of the large south window, and buttresses, including a trio along the south. No other changes

Exterior from the west: abbey on the right

Interior looking east

Cholmley Pew and galleries

took place before the Reformation except for the insertion of a two-light, straight-headed window in the south-west corner of the chancel in the fifteenth century. It is now partly obscured by an outside staircase.

The post-Reformation history is one of adaptation for auditory purposes. We begin with one minor seventeenth century addition; the plain, straight-headed and mullioned window in the centre of the chancel south wall. The north transept was remodelled in 1744 and given a group of three stepped 'lancets' in its north wall. It has a wooden outside staircase on the east side giving access to the gallery. The south transept was altered, though less drastically, in 1759. Its new west windows are, this time, round-headed, its east windows just plain rectangles. All have intersecting glazing bars, the *leitmotif* of these Georgian insertions. There is a boarded staircase on the west side, and in the re-entrant angle between transept and chancel is a second staircase for the Cholmley pew. This, with its Gothick-cum-Chinoiserie handrail could also be of 1759. The tracery of the large medieval south window was taken out and wooden Y-tracery put in its place. The transformation continued about 1764 with the insertion of four large, entirely domestic windows in the nave south wall. Two are exceptionally tall and all possess the glazing bars as above. A break then followed until 1818, when the whole north side was opened out and a wide north aisle built. It is broadly cross-gabled and has tall, pointed windows that are superficially Gothick. More emphatically Gothick is the south porch, built in 1821-3 to shelter the new entrance. It has an ogee arch on triple shafts, all thin and bamboo-like.

The visitor enters now under the west gallery and will be overwhelmed by what he sees. For this interior is unique in England and, indeed, bears little relation to the normal conception of a church. Surrounded as one is by so much panelling, one feels as if among the decks of a great wooden ship. The roof, one will not be surprised to learn, was in fact built by ships' carpenters. It is panelled and boarded and provided with skylights just as they occur on the deck of a ship. Down below in the hold, the visitor wends his way shoulder high among the pews which must be the envy of every child who wishes the church to be his own private playground. High above rises the pulpit, not dominant here as it would be in any other church. Then there occurs that crowning touch, the stove, with its flue shooting straight as a die up through the roof. The conversion of the medieval interior to its present state runs as follows. Late seventeenth century, Cholmley pew; 1700 west gallery; 1744 gallery in north transept; 1759 gallery in south transept; 1764 nave south gallery; 1818 north gallery and west balcony. The galleries are characterised by wavy divisions between the sets of seats. All are numbered and painted white. The box pews date variously from the seventeenth century to the early nineteenth century; they are stained a dark brown. The arcades, if they can be called that, date from the 1818 enlargement. They possess broad, flattened-out and panelled arches on sexfoiled piers trying hard to be Gothick, but in the end hardly succeeding. They have shafts with rings, capitals with acanthus-cum-crocket leaf, and thin, square abaci. All this upper woodwork is painted cream. The most singular item among this whole *ensemble* is the Cholmley pew placed irreverently across the chancel arch, an arrangement unique now, but once more common (eg, High Wycombe, Buckinghamshire). The twisted columns are copied from later seventeenth century monuments which, in turn, descend from Baroque Rome and Raphael cartoons.

The chancel, dark and mysterious beyond the Cholmley pew, plays no part in the quintessence of Whitby. It has its own private ambience and looks inwards. It is essentially Norman, with the rere-arches enlivened by a continuous roll and the chancel arch with fine rolls, a billet hood-mould (two with heads). The Norman windows in the nave have rere-arches, with nook-shafts and chevron. Finally, the tower arch, concealed by the vestibule, has waterleaf capitals; they confirm the date. So there we have it, a church full of interest — architectural, historical, social; a church which will keep the visitor occupied for many happy hours; a church whose nuances must be savoured at leisure.

Communion rail: Late C16; with sturdy turned balusters.
Communion table: Late C16; heavy turned legs; top with a band of hoops.
Box pews: C17; plain panelling; knobs.
Family pew: C17; on left of chancel arch; top strapwork frieze.
Cholmley pew: Late C17; projecting centre on four barley-sugar columns carrying Corinthian capitals; panels with garlanded surrounds; frieze of cherubs' heads below; top frieze of acanthus.
West gallery: 1700; plain panelling separated by fluted pilasters; stairs with slim turned balusters.
Commandment boards: C18; with raised lunette tops.
Box pews: C18-early C19; plain panelling.
North transept gallery: 1744; on Tuscan columns; front as west gallery.
South transept gallery: 1759; of differing heights; on wooden posts; fronts as west gallery but with a miniature balustrade on top.
Nave gallery: 1764; as north transept gallery.
Family pew: 1768; on right of chancel arch; plain panelling.
Chandelier: 1769; two tiers of branches; Baroque stem: an anchor at the top.
Clock: c1770; wavy surround with a coat of arms.
Pulpit (with tester): 1778; a three-decker; pulpit with ogee-headed panels; tester on quarterfoil shafts with leaf capitals; tester with frieze of interlaced arches and openwork canopy with curly ribs carrying a pineapple finial; reader's and clerk's desks with ogee-headed panelling; also a larger attached pew with miniature balustrade; two vamping horns on the back.
North aisle gallery: 1818; as north transept.
West balcony: 1818; on broad segmental arches with quarterfoiled spandrels; quarterfoil columns; balustrade.
Royal Arms: 1840; of Queen Victoria.

Beauchief

Exterior from the north-east

Box pew: detail

Beauchief is an odd-looking church and possesses a singularly odd history. In this it shares a certain rapport with Dale, but in other ways, partly visual, partly in spirit, the two churches stand worlds apart. The setting is deceptively rural. To the south-west wooded parkland flows up a hill; to the north-east the smooth folds of a golf course undulate into the distance. The forecourt is a trim lawn with flower beds flanked by a neat terrace of stone cottages. Yet, a few hundred yards to the north all is Sheffield suburbia, the endless waves of semis reducing the landscape to a formless monotony. The churchyard is beautifully managed, with the wall clad in vegetation partly bordering it on the south, and the lawn interspersed with clumps of wildness.

The first impression of the church is of a massive tower obscuring whatever lies behind. This tower is the only medieval part of the building, though clearly altered — in fact, it has lost a good third of its original height as well as the tracery of the main window. The tracery was, it seems, of the flowing type, the type with those organic, swaying forms much favoured about 1330-40. But the tower itself is a century older. It has sturdy angle buttresses with gabled set-offs, the latter enriched by blank trefoils which look later in style than the doorway below. The buttresses end now in plain, sawn-off tips, giving the tower a very blunt aspect. There is a squat pyramid roof, only visible from some distance away. The doorway has an arch with three keeled rolls and also five orders of moulded capitals suspended in mid-air, as it were, above the

space left vacant by the long lost shafts. The abaci are still square. Round the corner to the north is a fourteenth-century doorway with an ogee arch carrying a leaf finial and also two continuous keeled rolls. Left and right of the tower occur two re-set doorways, the left of about 1200, the right of the fourteenth century. This tower was the culmination of a building campaign which began during the late twelfth century, the campaign of a Premonstratensian abbey founded about 1175. The church was two hundred feet long, but of that only the high roof-line against the east wall of the tower remains. Also to be seen here is the tower arch pushing up above the present roof, a curious effect.

At the Dissolution, the church was allowed to fall into ruin, its walls no doubt used as a convenient quarry by local builders. By the accession of Charles II nothing substantial remained except the tower. About 1662 Edward Pegge, who had married into the Strelley family, erected a chapel against the east wall of the tower. It appears not to incorporate any fragments of the abbey church, certainly nothing in the way of details. In fact, the new chapel is devoid of any features save one, viz, the large four-light east window with its plain, Gothic Revival intersecting tracery.

The interior contains one spacial surprise impossible to anticipate from a perambulation of the exterior. The nave projects into the tower and has its own west wall with doorway and window independent of the real west wall beyond. So one first enters a small vestibule in the space that is left, a vestibule

Box pew: detail

which also serves as the baptistry. Looked at from the nave, it all appears as something of a muddle. The high and wide thirteenth-century tower arch is partly obscured by plastered walling. It has triple-chamfered responds and moulded capitals. The interior is a strange vessel, higher and wider than one would have supposed, with a formal atmosphere totally unlike the happy-go-lucky accumulations at Dale. Dark stained furnishings and orange-yellow walls impart a rich, surprisingly emotional atmosphere more Laudian than Protestant. The pulpit, too, is not quite so Puritan in its positioning as Dale's, being on the north side of the altar rather than behind. The roof is unceiled, and that is typical of the seventeenth century rather than the eighteenth which preferred plastered ceilings. The members are characteristically thin and include tie-beams, queenposts and collar beams. Also of note is the charming little psalm board, with its hooks to hang the numbers on and the box attached to the back where the numbers are stored. It seems to be unique.

Finally, some unfortunate detractions. They are principally the radiators and the plastic imitation hessian covering the carpet. The latter, surely, is hardly necessary.

Font: C17; octagonal; bowl with ogee quarterfoils; moulded stem.
Box pews: c1662, as are all the following; plain panelling; one block has finials with shields and knobs; one pew has three panels with heraldic devices.
Communion table: With heavy turned legs; the top with flowers in strapwork surrounds; has it been altered?
Cupboard: With pierced Gothic motifs including lancets and 'plate tracery'; is this original or made up?
Family pew: Tall; plain panelling; finial as box pews.
Pulpit: A three-decker; plain panelling and also upper panels with leaf designs in relief; book-rest on flat, wavy brackets; reader's and clerk's desks with panels as above. Also one hatchment. The communion rail looks recent.

Lead

Lead church, tiny and self-effacing, stands all alone in the middle of a large field, surrounded by the remnants of its churchyard. Lonely, and awaiting an uncertain future, its only companions are the cattle which browse nonchalently back and forth across the flat expansiveness. The churchyard has merged again into the field on the south and west sides, but eastwards there remains a wild, nettle-strewn patch shaded by trees and encompassed by a broken-down fence. It is a brooding, melancholy spot, haunted by a fear of abandonment, clinging desperately to some shadow of its former glory. The ragged trees behind add force to the prevailing mood of despondency.

The church, hardly a church, more the humblest of chapels, is built of irregular stones and consists of a single-celled nave-cum-chancel. A powerful and characterful bellcote rides on the west gable; it has a plain, pointed opening for the bell. There are diagonal buttresses of one set-off at the corners of the church and the gables above are quite strongly capped. The south doorway has continuous mouldings. The east and west windows are of two cusped lights with reticulated tracery. The north and south walls possess one window each. They are straight-headed and have two cusped ogee lights. These windows contain plate glass probably of the restoration which took place during the 1930s. It is regrettable, though eminently preferable to the nullifying effect of Victorian glass as it occurs at, for example, Glynde in Sussex. The date of the chapel is confirmed by the reticulated tracery; it is about 1320.

The interior is incredibly moving, not in the strict 'prayer-book' sense, but in being just timelessly unrestored and almost undatable, or rather asking not to be analysed in a clinical historicist way. It breathes exactly the same kind of atmosphere as Up Marden in Sussex. The interior is a single space, no larger than an average-sized drawing room. Although some may not approve of the bare stone walls, they seem to enhance the basic simplicity. Of architectural features, there exists only the roof, with tie-beams, kingposts and two-way struts. It could be seventeenth century. So interest can concentrate variously upon the stone altar incorporating what is probably the original *mensa*, a truly rustic set of benches, a little pulpit in the north-east corner, several text boards, and the stone floor. The altar also has a re-set coffin lid with a foliated cross and there are more in the floor. It is sad to note among all this perfection the redundancy notices posted up. What will happen to Lead if this goes through? Gradual decay and dereliction? A shed for the farmer's cattle or hay? It is ironic that the church should have received a thorough

Exterior from the south-east

To Do Good and also to
Distrebvte Forget not
For with svch sacrifices
God is well pleased Heb
the 13 ver the 16

Interior looking north-east

Wall plaque

overhaul in the 1930s and that today it still stands in excellent order. It is imperative that Lead be transferred to the Redundant Churches Fund; we can ill afford to lose such a charming building. It is no exaggeration to say that few other churches in England display so patently the loving faith and care of generations.

The furnishings are most likely to be of the C17.
Benches: Plain; open backs; plain ends with curly tops.
Plaques: Two oval ones with texts and re-used C15 leaf bosses.
Pulpit: A three-decker; plain panelling; clerk's desk with square finials carrying little pyramids.
Text boards: Plain; with biblical quotations.

Midhopestones

Midhopestones is a grey village of stone houses and cottages clinging to the south side of the Don Valley. From the opposite slopes the church appears hardly distinguishable among the various buildings and stands out only after one has pinpointed the churchyard. The landscape is hard and gritty, the bare moors with their criss-cross of stone walls enclosing on all sides. Leafyness is confined to the valley bottom. Only the disfiguring line of pylons reminds one of industrial Sheffield a few miles to the south-east. The church is placed at the apex of the village, hard by a farmyard, and consequently enjoys the finest views. Down below, a reservoir provides reflective relief from the swelling, grey-green hills. The churchyard lies on a slope, large and windswept, with the church at the foot and pines, etc, higher up. It makes the already tiny church appear even smaller.

Midhopestones church is indeed small; it cannot be much larger than Lead, consisting of a single nave and chancel, though with the addition of a south porch. It is built of stone and has a lovely stone slated roof. Note the perfect graduation in the size of the slates from eaves to apex, so different to the monotonous regularity of modern imitation tiles. The porch entrance has a flattened-depressed arch under a straight hood-mould. Above is a coat of arms in a plain frame, and the gable carries a ball finial. The south doorway repeats the motifs of the porch entrance; the mouldings of both are all very 'debased'. The west, south and east windows are three-lighters with plain mullions and straight heads. The chancel north window, and also an upper west window, have two lights instead, but are otherwise identical. On the west gable reposes a pretty bellcote with a plain, rectangular opening for the bell and an openwork cresting with heavy diagonal ribs supporting another ball finial. The date, which can be read above the porch doorway, will come as a surprise after this description: 1705. For here is a church which could be of 1605 or 1625, judging by its motifs, which are unequivocally Gothic Survival. There is nothing to suggest that Wren's City churches ever existed, let alone the Baroque of the early eighteenth century. It graphically illustrates how behind-the-times its builders were; yet this occurrence of a stylistic time-lag between the central, London, events and the remoter provinces is by no means unique. The church was built by Godfrey Bosville, High Sheriff of the county, who had acquired the manor in 1690. It is his crest which appears above the porch entrance.

The interior is delightfully small-scaled and domestic, though differing markedly from Lead, not only in the character of its furnishings but also in the moods which it evokes. There is less here of that timelessness which is the hallmark of Lead, more of an adaptation to continuing usage. Less formal than Beauchief, it nevertheless has something of the plushness of that church. Everything is well looked after, from the new red carpets to the perfectly acceptable modern light fittings. Among the furnishings the gallery dominates, as also does the light from the windows, the latter dazzling punctuations in an interior predominantly of darker hues. Of especial interest are two pews still bearing the names of those who rented them, Sarah Wainwright and John Wilson. The cambered roof has collar beams and is ceiled between the rafters. The plaster is painted a deep orange, a striking effect which adds to the richness. The walls, conversely, are a reticent white. Altogether, Midhopestones is a remarkably late example of a church designed and furnished in the Jacobean tradition, and it is heartening to see that proper care is being taken of it.

All furnishings are of c1705.

Box pews: Plain panelling; knobs; two with names of pew renters.

Pulpit: Three tiers of panelling; lower with lozenge in a star; middle with enriched blank arches; upper with a pair of enriched guilloche motifs; back-post ditto. The pulpit may be early seventeenth century and re-used from the medieval church, which was its predecessor.

Wall panelling: Ditto.

West gallery: On two thin posts and two brackets; font with plain lower panelling and a deep balustrade with turned balusters; stairs in two flights with turned balusters.

Box pew door

Gallery staircase

Tong

Exterior from the south-west

Interior looking west

Tong lies in the centre of that precious rural enclave between the sordid urbanization of Bradford and Leeds. How long it will remain undefiled is a debatable point. As it is, church, hall and cottages stand together within a leafy framework at the west end of the village. The church forms the centrepiece, as the hall lies back behind a rich belt of trees, though its garden comes right down to the road. To the right, a cottage is placed transversely, closing the east view and pointing across the road to another cottage and a farm building. The latter has attached to it the inevitable detracting modern extensions. The domesticity of the cottages contrasts effectively with the more formal lines of the church. The churchyard is formal, too, with its aspirant gateway and the rectangular tombs including a blackened obelisk.

The church was built, or rather rebuilt, in 1727. A few furtive features survive from the medieval building, mainly round at the back so that nothing will disturb the 'new look' Georgian facade as it appears from the road. These facades are of a dark ashlar, soot-blackened in places, flaking here and there, the victim of industrial pollution. The plan consists of a west tower, a nave, a north aisle, and a chancel. Of medieval features the following show externally. The tower west window incorporates re-used two-light Perpendicular tracery and the three north aisle windows are early sixteenth century, as their two plain arched lights under a straight hood-mould indicate. That leaves the three-light chancel east window, also Perpendicular, but looking over-restored now. Is it original, or is it a Victorian replacement of a Georgian window? One would expect a Middle-Pointed design, rather than a Perpendicular one, from the Victorians. Alternatively, it could be a particularly accurate early nineteenth-century insertion. It does, however, contain Victorian glass.

The rest is all 1727. It will be noted that no attempt has been made to give the south side a symmetrical facade as it was done at, for example, Gayhurst. The placing of a truncated window above a doorway at the west end of the south side is familiar from Pilling and, on a much grander scale, All Saints at Oxford. The west tower is of two stages and has panelled angle pilasters, a parapet with urns, a round-arched west window, an upper circular, keyed-in west window, and plain, round-arched bell-openings with keystone. The side windows are large and round-arched with panelled surrounds, keystones, and block-like abaci. The south doorway is the same but the priest's doorway has a straight lintel instead.

It is pleasant to be able to conclude our excursion into the realm of 'prayer-book' churches with such an attractive interior as this. Clear, light and crisp, and logically organised, only the glass in the east window and the shabby, peeling walls detract. The latter, at least, could be remedied. Otherwise there are box pews everywhere, taller family pews, a gallery, flat ceilings, and a good three-decker. The font cover, with its urn balanced upon a baluster, is exquisite and amusing. From the medieval period survive the arches of the north arcade, fourteenth century, double-chamfered, and made round instead of pointed when the arcade was rebuilt. They rest now upon elegantly slim Tuscan columns carrying prominent square abaci. The arcade is three bays long. Attached to the columns are pretty lamps suspended from little brackets. The flat nave ceiling has a central roundel with a fan-like surround. The chancel has a plaster barrel vault and both are painted blue. An untouched interior is always a thrilling experience and here at Tong we are doubly grateful for its survival in an area whose buildings are predominantly nineteenth century.

Box pew: C17; in the south-west corner; panels with S-shaped arabesque; one knob; possibly made up.
Nave panelling: C17; panels with S-shaped arabesque; re-used.
Box pews: 1727, as are all the following; plain panelling; numbered; arranged college-wise in the aisle and raised theatrically.
Chancel panelling: Plain.
Communion rail: Slim turned balusters carrying square entablature sections.
Communion table: Thin turned legs.
Family pews: Rising concavely; plain panelling; that on the north side has a fireplace.
Font: Gadrooned bowl; plain circular stem; moulded base.
Font Cover: Circular, flat base; fluted urn on a baluster which in turn stands on a circular base supported by a central Tuscan column and four volute brackets.
Pulpit (with tester): A three-decker; plain panelling; plain panelled back-post; tester with segmentally-raised sections to cornice.
West gallery: On square posts; plainly panelled front.
Royal Arms: 1760; of George III; lozenge-shaped.
Text boards: Early C19(?); arched panels; texts arranged under painted two-light trefoiled canopies with an encirled trefoil above; Ten Commandments, Creed and Lord's Prayer.
Also six hatchments.

The font cover

Gazetteer

The churches included here are of two kinds; firstly, those with completely unrestored or prayer-book interiors which for reasons of space and selection could not be accommodated in the main part of the book, and secondly those with prayer-book interiors marred by later alterations. Those in the first group are indicated thus: *. In addition, there exist many churches with odd sets of box pews, the occasional gallery, so-called Jacobean pulpits, etc. Their furnishings are otherwise arranged according to the tenets of the Camdenians. Such churches cannot be listed here and must be sought among the pages of the *Buildings of England*.

BERKSHIRE

Besselsleigh* Tiny C12-C15/C17 church with complete C17/C18 furnishings. Box pews, communion rail & table, font, gallery, pulpit, tympanum.

BUCKINGHAMSHIRE

Biddlesden* 1731. Built into the stables of the house. Interior somewhat disjointed. Benches, communion rail, font, hatchments, pulpit, royal arms, text boards, wall panelling, west gallery.

Thornton Rebuilt c1850 but retaining prayer-book furnishings, probably of the early C19. Box pews, two-decker pulpit, squire's pew, west gallery.

Willen 1679-80, but apse added 1861. Recently beautifully restored with new clear glass, etc. Late C17 box pews, communion table, font with cover, stalls, two-decker pulpit, wall panelling.

CHESHIRE

Baddiley* Medieval timber-framed church partly cased in brick in 1811. Perfect interior, a little untidy, with C17/C18 furnishings. Benches, box pews, communion rail & table, three-decker pulpit, screen & tympanum, west gallery.

Congleton 1740-2. C17/C18 furnishings. Some alterations. Cut-down box pews, chandelier, three-sided communion rail, font & cover, three galleries, centrally-placed pulpit, reredos, royal arms, wall paintings.

Shotwick C12-C16 church with C17/C18 furnishings. Box pews, chancel panelling, chandelier, churchwardens' pew, communion rail & table, three-decker pulpit, royal arms.

Threapwood 1815. Good interior but with some changes (eg, pulpit moved from west end). Benches, box pews, chandeliers, three-sided communion rail, family pews, font, three galleries, pulpit, reredos.

CUMBERLAND

Whitehaven 1752-3, with contemporary furnishings. Some alterations. Cut-down box pews, communion rail, font with cover, three galleries, pulpit, reredos, screens.

DERBYSHIRE

Foremark* 1662, with contemporary furnishings. Box pews, chancel panelling, communicants' pews, communion rail &

Whitehaven, Cumberland: *Pulpit*

table, font with cover, hatchments, three-decker pulpit, royal arms, screen.

Trusley Early C18. Near-perfect interior spoilt by Victorian and later glass. Box pews, chancel panelling, communion rail & table, font with cover, hatchments, three-decker pulpit, royal arms.

DEVON

Branscombe Fine C12-C15 church with a good selection of C17/C18 furnishings. Box pews, three-sided communion rail, communion table, hatchment, three-decker pulpit, screen, west gallery.

Cruwys Morchard Medieval church with many prayer-book furnishings of the early C18. Benches, box pews, churchwardens' pew, three-sided communion rail, family pew, font cover, plaster wall panelling, pulpit, screen.

Exeter (St Martin) Late medieval church with C17/C18 furnishings. Some later changes. Box pews, communicants' seats, three-sided communion rail, pulpit, reredos, west gallery.

Molland* Late medieval church with perfect interior. C17-early C19 furnishings. Baptismal pew, box pews, childrens' pews, Commandment boards, communion rail & table, family pew, three-decker pulpit, royal arms, screen & tympanum.

West Ogwell Church of c1300 with C17-early C19 furnishings. Benches, box pews, communion rail, parlour pew, pulpit, royal arms, wall panelling. Under threat of redundancy.

DORSET

Blandford Forum 1733-9, but with a chancel of 1896. Otherwise almost unaltered. Late C17-late C18 furnishings. Benefaction boards, box pews, Commandment boards, font with cover, mayor's chair, organ, pulpit, royal arms, wall panelling, west gallery.

Charlton Marshall C15 & 1713. Early C18 furnishings. Cut-down box pews, communion rail, font with cover, pulpit, reredos, royal arms, wall panelling.

Folke 1628. Many original furnishings, in fact almost complete. Benches, communion rail & table, font with cover, hatchments, hourglass stand, lectern, pulpit, screen, stalls, wall panelling.

Puddletown C12-C15, with chancel of 1910-1. Good nave ensemble with Carolean furnishings. Box pews, churchwardens' pew, three-sided communion rail, font cover, painted texts, two-decker pulpit, squire's pew, west gallery.

West Stafford C15-1640. Chancel 1898. C17/C18 furnishings. Benches, chandelier, communion rail, pulpit, royal arms, screen, west gallery.

Molland, Devon: *Royal Arms*

DURHAM

Brancepeth★ Medieval church partly rebuilt and refurnished c1626-65. Remarkable Gothic furnishings essentially complete. Benches, chancel panelling, clock, communion rail & table, family pews, font with canopy, hatchments, nave panelling, two-decker pulpit, reredos, screen, stalls.

Haughton-le-Skerne Medieval church refurnished in the C17. Some Victorian changes. Box pews, canopies, chancel panelling, communion rail, font with cover, hatchments, nave panelling, twin pulpit & reader's desk, reredos, royal arms.

ESSEX

Wanstead★ 1787-90, with contemporary furnishings. Perfect interior marred only by Victorian glass. Box pews, chancel rail, communion rail & table, font, three galleries, pulpit.

GLOUCESTERSHIRE

Didmarton Medieval & C18. C18 furnishings, but also some Victorian benches replacing one block of pews. Box pews, communion rail, font cover, hat pegs, panelled window surrounds, three-decker pulpit, reredos. Not in a good state at the time of writing.

HAMPSHIRE

Boarhunt★ Saxon church of c1064 refurnished c1853 yet entirely in a prayer-book manner! Nothing altered since. Benches, communion rail & table, font, three-decker pulpit, squire's pew, west gallery.

Trusley, Derbyshire: *Font and cover*

Wanstead, Essex: *Monument and pulpit*

Idsworth C12 church with post-Reformation alterations. The interior, though appearing genuine, was made more prayer-bookish by Goodhart-Rendel in 1912. Benches, box pews, communion rail, pulpit, west gallery.
Southwick Gothic Survival church of 1566. Good set of C16-C18 furnishings alas ruined by replacement benches of the 1950s. Communion rail & table, family pews, three-decker pulpit, reredos, west gallery.

HEREFORDSHIRE

Abbey Dore Late C12-early C13 & C17. Refurnished 1634. Furnishings still extant but re-arranged. Almsbox, communion rail, pulpit, reader's desk, royal arms, screen, stained glass, stalls, west gallery.
Monnington-on-Wye Gothic Survival church of 1679. Almost untouched but the pulpit cut down and reduced to floor level. Benches, communion rail & table, font, pulpit, reader's desk, reredos, royal arms, screen, tower gates.
Stoke Edith★ C14 & 1740-2. Untouched interior with original C18 furnishings. Box pews, three-sided communion rail, font, three-decker pulpit, squire's pew, west gallery.
Tyberton 1719-21. Spoilt by Victorian Gothicised windows. Contemporary furnishings only slightly altered. Box pews, cut-down box pews, communion rail & table, font, hatchments, lamp standards, lectern, two-decker pulpit, reredos, royal arms.

Stapleford, Leicestershire

HERTFORDSHIRE

Stanstead Abbotts★ C15/late C16 church with essentially untouched interior. Box pews, communion rail & table, hatchments, three-decker pulpit, royal arms, text boards, tower screen. Threatened with redundancy.

HUNTINGDONSHIRE

Leighton Bromswold C13-C15 & 1634. Refurnished c1627-34. Some C19 restoration and importations. Benches, communion rail, font cover, twin pulpit & reader's desk, screen, stalls.
Little Gidding Tiny church of 1714. Furnishings of c1625/c1714. Some changes were made in 1853. Chancel panelling, communion table, font with cover, hourglass stand, lectern, reredos, stalls.

KENT

Old Romney C13-early C16 church with C18 furnishings. Some re-arrangement. Box pews, chancel gates, communion rail, pulpit, reader's desk, reredos, royal arms, text boards, west gallery.

LEICESTERSHIRE

Stapleford★ Gothick church of 1783 with all its original furnishings. Box pews set college-wise, three-sided communion rail & table, font, two-decker pulpit, reredos, west gallery.
Wistow C12-C15 & 1746. Near-perfect interior marred by some Victorian additions. Furnishings of c1746. Box pews, chancel panelling, communion rail, font, hatchment, pulpit, reredos, royal arms, screen.

LINCOLNSHIRE

Mareham-on-the-Hill Small church remodelled 1804. Furnishings mostly original but with recent additions. Box pews, communicants' benches, font, hatchment, two-decker pulpit.

NORFOLK

Bylaugh★ C14/C15 & 1809-10. Complete untouched interior of 1809. Box pews, chancel panelling, communion rail & table, family pews, font cover, hatchment, three-decker pulpit, reredos, royal arms.

Thurning Late C13-C15 church with furnishings of 1742. Spoilt by Victorian additions. Benches, box pews, chancel panelling, three-sided communion rail, communion table, three-decker pulpit.

Wilby C14/C15 church with many furnishings of c1633-8. Almsbox, benches, box pews, communion rail & table, three-decker pulpit, royal arms, screen, west gallery.

NORTHAMPTONSHIRE

Passenham C13-C15 & 1626. Remarkable furnishings of c1626-8. Spoilt by an ill-advised re-ordering in 1968. Box pews, communion table, pulpit, stalls, wall paintings, west gallery.

Plumpton A sweet little Gothick church of 1822. Good set of C17/early C19 funishings spoilt by some crass Victorian alterations. Benches, box pews, communion rail, font, reredos. In danger of redundancy.

NOTTINGHAMSHIRE

Teversal C12-C14 church with much work of c1675. Almost complete set of late C17 furnishings. Baptismal pew, box pews, communion rail & table, family pew, hatchments, two-decker pulpit, royal arms, stalls, west gallery.

Tythby Medieval church with C18 alterations. Also some Victorian work. Good set of C17/C18 furnishings. Box pews, Commandment boards, communion rail, family pews, font, two-decker pulpit, royal arms, screen, west gallery.

Winkburn★ C12/C13 church with C17/C18 furnishings. More-or-less complete. Box pews, chests, communion rail, family pew, font, pulpit, railings, reader's desk, royal arms, screen.

OXFORDSHIRE

Shorthampton Tiny C12-C15 church with good set of C17/C18 furnishings. Only a few changes. Box pews, communion table, font cover, hat pegs, painted texts, two-decker pulpit.

Waterperry C11-C15 church with C17/C18 furnishings. Box pews, chest, communion rail, family pews, pulpit, reader's desk, royal arms.

RUTLAND

Teigh★ Gothick church of 1782 with unique interior. Spoilt by a reconstruction of the windows in 1911. Box pews arranged college-wise, three-sided communion rail, communion table, font, pulpit & twin reader's desks set above west doorway, reredos, text boards, wall paintings.

SHROPSHIRE

Leebotwood Medieval church with C17/C18 furnishings. Some Victorian changes. Box pews, choir pews, family pews, font cover, two-decker pulpit, west gallery.

Longnor c1260-70. Many C18 furnishings. Some restoration. Box pews, three-sided communion rail, communion table, font cover, hatchments, two-decker pulpit, squire's pew, vicar's pew, west gallery.

Stokesay C12-C15 & 1654/64. Almost complete set of C17/C18 furnishings. Box pews, family pew, painted texts, three-decker pulpit, west gallery.

Teigh, Rutland

SOMERSET

Cameley Medieval church with good set of C17-early C19 furnishings. Some fussy later additions. Box pews, communion rail & table, family pew, font cover, two galleries, hat pegs, painted texts, pulpit, reader's desk, reredos, royal arms.

Catcott Medieval church with C17-early C19 furnishings. Spoilt by Victorian furnishings in the chancel. Benches with childrens' seats, communion rail & table, font cover, painted texts, pulpit, reader's desk, royal arms, text boards, west gallery.

Croscombe C14-early C16 church with a remarkable set of furnishings of 1616. Some Victorian restoration, glass, etc. Box pews, chandelier, pulpit, twin reader's and clerk's desks, royal arms, screen, stalls.

Holcombe Medieval church with characterful interior spoilt by Victorian chancel furnishings. C18/early C19 furnishings. Box pews, Commandment boards, two-decker pulpit, royal arms, west gallery.

Stawley C12-C15 church with C18 furnishings. Some suspect alterations. Box pews, Commandment boards, communion rail, pulpit, royal arms.

Wyke Champflower 1623-4. A strange little chapel attached to the house. Contemporary furnishings, very little altered. Box pews, chancel panelling, communion rail & table, font cover, lectern, pulpit, reredos, tympanum.

SUFFOLK

Kedington Late C13-C15 church with a wealth of C17-early C19 furnishings. Chancel panelling, childrens' benches, communicants' stalls, three-sided communion rail, family pews, hourglass stand, three-decker pulpit, screen, west gallery, wig stand.

Withersdale C12-C14 church. Good set of C17 furnishings marred by Victorian additions. Benches, box pews, communion rail & table, three-decker pulpit, reredos, west gallery.

SUSSEX

Ashburnham C15/1665. Many C17 furnishings. Some alterations. Cut-down box pews, three-sided communion rail, communion table, font with cover, pulpit, railings, former reredos, tower staircase, west gallery.

Chichester (St John) Octagonal church of 1812-3. Contemporary furnishings but, alas, all the pews replaced in 1879. Commandment boards, three-sided communion rail, galleries all round, centrally-placed three-decker pulpit. Future uncertain.

Glynde 1763-5. A perfect set of C18 furnishings completely ruined by the most obnoxious Victorian glass. Box pews, communion rail, font, pulpit, west gallery.

Parham* 1545/c1820. Perfect Gothick interior. Box pews, chancel panelling, chandelier, communion rail, font, parlour pew, two-decker pulpit, reredos, royal arms, screen, vicar's pew.

Penhurst Medieval & C17. A good set of C17/C18 furnishings. Some Victorian intrusions. Box pews, Commandment board, communion rail, pulpit, reader's desk, screen, wall panelling.

Up Marden Small C13 church. Not a prayer-book interior but full of unrestored character and atmosphere. Benches, box pews, communion rail.

WARWICKSHIRE

Castle Bromwich 1726-31. Good interior keeping all its original furnishings. Some restoration. Box pews, communion rail, font with cover, three-decker pulpit, reredos, squire's pew, vicar's pew, west gallery.

Honiley Pretty Baroque church of 1723. Very small. Original furnishings but some suspect alterations. Box pews, communion rail & table, pulpit, reredos, west gallery.

WESTMORLAND

Ravenstonedale 1738/44. Near-perfect interior marred by Victorian choir stalls, etc. Benches arranged college-wise, communion rail & table, font cover, three-decker pulpit, royal arms, text boards, west gallery.

WILTSHIRE

Alton Priors C12-C15. Beautifully restored by the Redundant Churches Fund with, yes, new box pews! Box pews, communion rail & table, stalls.

Farley 1689-90. Many original furnishings but also many changes and additions. Cut-down box pews, communion rail & table, font with cover, hatchments, pulpit, screens, wall panelling.

Foxley Late C12-C18 church. Homely interior with many C17/C18 furnishings. Cut-down box pews, communion rail & table, painted texts, pulpit, reredos, screen.

Ham Medieval & 1733. Various Victorian alterations, C18 furnishings. Box pews, communion rail & table, family pews, pulpit, west gallery.

Lydiard Tregoze C13-C15 church with an intriguing interior, not all of it original. C17/C18 furnishings. Box pews, communion rail, font cover, pulpit, reredos, royal arms, screen, stained glass.

Sherrington 1624, re-using medieval features. A small church keeping most of its original furnishings. Some changes. Benches, communion rail & table, font cover, painted texts, pulpit.

Stratford-sub-Castle C13-C15 & 1711. Near-perfect interior with furnishings of c1615, c1711 and c1800. Only a few changes. Cut-down box pews, communicants' pews, communion rail, hourglass, organ, pulpit, reredos, royal arms, screen, squire's pew, vicar's pew, wall panelling, west gallery.

Stratford Tony C13-C15. Good set of C17 furnishings. Some restoration. Benches, communion rail, two-decker pulpit, stalls, wall panelling.

YORKSHIRE (EAST RIDING)

York* (Holy Trinity, Goodramgate) C13-C15 church with an unaltered interior. C17/C18 furnishings. Box pews, three-sided communion rail, communion table, font with cover, two-decker pulpit, reredos, royal arms. Not used for services but preserved.

YORKSHIRE (WEST RIDING)

Aldfield* Small church of c1783 with a perfectly preserved interior. Contemporary furnishings. Box pews, Commandment boards, communion rail & table, font, three-decker pulpit.

Leeds (St John) 1632-4. Gothic Survival church with remarkable Carolean furnishings. Some unfortunate Victorian alterations. Baptistry rail, benches, three-sided communion rail, font cover, two-decker pulpit, royal arms, screen. Now looked after by the Redundant Churches Fund.

Slaidburn C14/C15 church with many furnishings of late C16-C18. Benefaction boards, benches, box pews, chest, former communion table, family pews, font cover, three-decker pulpit, royal arms, screen.

Leeds (St John): *Detail of cresting*

Appendix to Second Edition (correct to June 1989)

The following additions and corrections have come to light since the first edition was published in 1979.

Tushingham Old Church, Cheshire
A chapel existed here in 1349. The small brick building in the churchyard is a former hearse-house built in 1834. It now contains the original hearse of 1880 restored recently and observable through a specially inserted window. The gallery and its access appear to be of shortly after 1821 as in that year the then owner of the manor, Daniel Vawdrey, offered to pay for its construction. The furnishings are of Cheshire oak. The rushes (not straw) are laid down only for Rushbearing Sunday and are removed soon afterwards.

Dale, Derbyshire
Technically, Dale is not, and has never been, a parish church. The gallery access from the 'infirmary' was closed several generations ago. Access is thus provided only by the external stair which is used occasionally.

Easton (St George Reforne), Dorset
The westward-facing pews are not unique after all; several other churches (eg Skelton and Robin Hood's Bay) also retain examples.

Leweston, Dorset
The school is Independent and so the remarks in the final paragraph no longer apply.

Winterborne Tomson, Dorset
The gallery incorporates woodwork from the former medieval screen.

Little Washbourne, Gloucestershire
The nave roof is almost entirely modern.

Clodock, Herefordshire
The boarded roofs are indeed of 1916-19 but the main beams are medieval. The chancel roof was opened up in 1980. There exists also a thirteenth-century 'dug-out' chest.

Shobdon, Herefordshire
The authorship of the C18 reconstruction remains obscure. The building and its contents may have been designed by William Kent, but there is a possibility that Thomas Farnolls Pritchard of Shrewsbury may have been involved. Since Kent died in 1748 Pritchard may have supervised the building's erection and fitting out. However, this is tentative and must not be regarded as anything more than that.

Stelling, Kent
Scientific investigation recently proved that one of the yew trees is approximately fifteen hundred years old!

Pilling Old Church, Lancashire
Now vested in the Redundant Churches Fund and thus no longer in disrepair. Sadly, the communion table has been stolen; a local craftsman has replaced it. The pulpit is a two, not a three, decker.

Chislehampton, Oxfordshire
The pulpit and some roof timbers come from the predecessor church which stood on a different site. The chandeliers are late nineteenth-century copies; the originals are now in the USA.

Brooke, Rutland
The stone slates are Colleywestons. The north door's hinges may be mid-thirteenth-century work. There exists also a medieval chest.

Hardington, Somerset
Another opinion assigns the south doorway to the late eighteenth century.

Ingestre, Staffordshire
The roadway has been metalled and the nineteenth-century stable restored to use. The extant pews are not true box pews; they are Victorian reconstruction (before 1886 when electric lighting was installed).

Shelland, Suffolk
The church had previously been rebuilt in 1646. The present colour scheme dates from 1896 and was originally executed by the local wainwright in imitation of wagon colour schemes. A repainting in 1971 employed slightly more pastel shades. The font is of the fourteenth century. The organ is a true barrel organ and is believed to be the only one in the world still in regular use! It was made by Bryceson of London about 1810.

Warminghurst, Sussex
Now preserved by the Redundant Churches Fund. The south porch has been cleared of vegetation. The pulpit is a two, not a three, decker.

Inglesham, Wiltshire
The Dutch barn has been taken down.

Mildenhall, Wiltshire
A major restoration took place during 1980-2 after the discovery of dry and wet rot.

Old Dilton, Wiltshire
There is some doubt as to the authenticity of the font; it may be C19. The clockmaker's name is Cockey, not Cook.

Robin Hood's Bay, Yorkshire
This church is more properly known as Fylingdales. It is now vested in the Redundant Churches Fund. The chancel with its buttresses may date from the seventeenth century and was thus only modified in 1821. The font is seventeenth century.

The 'seaweed' hangings are in fact those rare survivals, maidens' garlands!

Skelton Old Church, Yorkshire
One of the rescue stories of the decade. Saved, at last, by the Redundant Churches Fund and no longer derelict.

Whitby, Yorkshire
The vamping horns are, in fact, voice horns used by the hard-of-hearing.

Lead, Yorkshire
No longer a worry as it has been vested in the Redundant Churches Fund. The immediate surroundings have been tidied up.

Midhopestones, Yorkshire
A re-ordering took place in 1979. It included levelling the chancel floor and the installation of a neo-Jacobean communion table. The nave floor is now stone-flagged and the ceiling has also been painted white. The work of 1705 represents a rebuilding, not a completely new church. In a litigation case of shortly before this date, the church was described as 'broken down'.

Tong, Yorkshire
A major repair job was undertaken in 1979. It involved removing all the furnishings which were conserved and eventually returned exactly as before. Excavation revealed traces of a Saxon predecessor of the present church. Also medieval is the present tower arch completely concealed by organ and gallery. This is Norman, probably of before 1140, and was originally the chancel arch. It was moved in 1727 and extensively modified. The gallery itself was probably erected in 1731. The churchwardens' pew (in the south-west corner) bears the date 1628.

Whitehaven, Cumberland
The magnificent Georgian pulpit was, some years ago and against all opinion, wantonly mutilated. Now cut down to ground level, it remains yet another shocking indictment of the Church of England's refusal to countenance full planning controls over churches and their contents.

West Ogwell, Devon
Now vested in the Redundant Churches Fund.

Didmarton, Gloucestershire
Now vested in the Redundant Churches Fund.

Stanstead Abbotts, Hertfordshire
Now vested in the Redundant Churches Fund.

Goltho, Lincolnshire
As with Skelton one can now report a happy ending to a very sad story. When I visited it in 1977 Goltho stood derelict and abused with all furnishings removed. Rescued by the Redundant Churches Fund, the furnishings are now being reinstated (June 1989). A dear little brick church (nave about 1640, chancel sixteenth century) standing alone in a field. Box pews, communion rail, two-decker pulpit, reredos.

Babington, Somerset
A crashing omission from the first edition! A perfect little Georgian church standing by itself upon the vast front lawn of the house. Built in 1750 it retains an absolutely untouched interior. Box pews, wrought-iron communion rail, communion table, panelling, pulpit, reredos.

Cameley, Somerset
Now vested in the Redundant Churches Fund.

Holcombe, Somerset
Now preserved by the Redundant Churches Fund.

Chichester (St John), Sussex
Now vested in the Redundant Churches Fund. The organ is original also.

Alton Priors, Wiltshire
The box pews are not new after all but simply the original ones conserved and repainted.

Stratford Tony, Wiltshire
Now vested in the Redundant Churches Fund.

Worcester (St Swithun), Worcestershire
Omitted from the first edition. A fine Georgian town church built 1734-6 and possibly designed by the Woodwards of Chipping Campden. Untouched interior with wrought-iron communion table, font, box pews, commanding three-decker pulpit, west gallery, mayor's throne.

York (Holy Trinity), Yorkshire
Now vested in the Redundant Churches Fund.